PLAYBACK+
Speed • Pitch • Balance • Loop

Transcriptions • Les...

MW00817248

25 GREAT JAZZ SOLOS

Featuring Jazz Piano Legends Chick Corea, Duke Ellington, Bill Evans, Erroll Garner, Herbie Hancock, Keith Jarrett, Oscar Peterson, Bud Powell, Art Tatum, McCoy Tyner, and Many More

By Huw White

To access audio visit:
www.halleonard.com/mylibrary

Enter Code
8077-3167-1384-0427

ISBN 978-1-4803-9495-7

HAL•LEONARD®
CORPORATION
7777 W. BLUEMOUND RD. P.O. BOX 13819 MILWAUKEE, WI 53213

Visit Hal Leonard Online at
www.halleonard.com

Preface

25 Great Jazz Piano Solos is a collection of transcriptions, re-recordings and analyses of seminal solo performances by 25 of the greatest jazz pianists in history. While there are many hugely important and influential jazz pianists who don't appear on the list, effort was made to choose 25 pianists and performances that would best give an overview of the history and development of the idiom from the late swing era, through the birth and development of bebop, cool and modal jazz, into the "Young Lions" movement of the late 20th century. Though each of the chosen pianists has a vast and diverse body of work of their own, in many cases demonstrating significant variation in individual style as their careers developed, the solos were chosen to best represent what might be considered as each pianist's "classic" style at a particular snapshot in time, while fitting into the chronological narrative of the book.

As for the song choices themselves, many were already considered at the time (or have since become adopted) as "standards" within the unofficial but universally acknowledged canon of the Great American Songbook. Others are original compositions by either the pianists themselves, their bandmates and contemporaries, or their own jazz heroes. In many cases these originals have now become part of the extended working repertoire of the modern jazz musician. A good number of the selection are blues, deliberately so, in acknowledgement of the fundamental importance of that singular musical form within the jazz tradition, and to document the development of its soloistic treatment as an important sub-narrative.

Throughout the book, chord symbols are given to point to both the underlying song harmony and the pianist's improvisational interpretation of the harmony. In many cases, re-harmonizations and implied or superimposed harmonies are given in brackets. Frequently, the improvised performances stretch the limits of practical theoretical analysis, and in these instances the chord symbols given are either subjective, and therefore open to personal interpretation, or left out altogether. As always with music, what the ears learn to recognize and interpret, and what the body learns to assimilate and create, are eventually more important than the theoretical processes that help kick start our understanding in the mind. It is the author's hope that the tools provided in this book help to open up for the reader and student a world of exploration, discovery, and ultimately, personal expression within the galaxy of jazz piano and the universe of music.

–Huw White

About the Online Audio

There are two online audio versions for each solo: 1) a demo track with the solo piano; 2) a backing track without the solo piano. These allow you to hear how the solo sounds, and provide an opportunity to play it along with the rhythm track. The time code shown at the start of each transcribed excerpt indicates the point where the solo begins on the source recording. Though the audio tracks attempt to replicate the original performances, there is no substitute for the real thing. In most instances, you can find these online, so please search them out and listen.

The music on the audio tracks is performed by:

Huw White   piano
Tom Farmer   double bass
Josh Morales   drums

Recorded at Novelty Box Studios, London, UK
Engineered by Joshua Morales
Produced and mixed by Huw White

Contents

Count Basie

William P. Gottlieb collection/Library of Congress

"If you play a tune and a person don't tap their feet, don't play the tune."

–Count Basie

Count Basie led his orchestra for nearly half a century, from 1935 until his death in 1984. He introduced several generations of listeners to the Big Band sound, helping to shape the course of jazz and popular music in the mid-20th century, leaving behind a highly influential catalogue of music. In 1958, he became the first African-American male to win a Grammy Award, garnering many more throughout his illustrious career.

Born on August 21, 1904 in Red Bank, New Jersey, William James "Count" Basie was given his first piano lessons by his mother. Basie dreamed of a traveling life, inspired by touring carnivals that came to town. He finished junior high school, but spent much of his time doing occasional chores at the Palace Theater in Red Bank to gain free admission to performances. He quickly learned how to improvise piano music to fit the acts and silent movies.

By the age of 15, Basie was playing with pick-up groups for dances and amateur shows. Around 1920 he went to Harlem, where he met Willie "The Lion" Smith and James P. Johnson. By the time he was 20 years old, Basie had toured extensively as a solo pianist, accompanist, and music director for blues singers, dancers, and comedians, providing an early training that was to prove significant later.

Count Basie

Back in Harlem in 1925, Basie gained his first steady playing job at Leroy's, where the band "winged" every number without sheet music. Around the same time, he met Fats Waller, who taught him organ. As with Duke Ellington, Willie "The Lion" Smith helped Basie out by arranging him gigs, introducing him to musicians, and teaching him piano.

Basie toured in several acts between 1925 and 1927 on the burlesque and vaudeville circuits, taking him to Kansas City, St. Louis, New Orleans, and Chicago. He met many jazz musicians on these tours, including Louis Armstrong. In 1928, Basie joined Walter Page and his Famous Blue Devils, one of the first big bands, which played mostly in Texas and Oklahoma. It was around this time that he began to be known as "Count" Basie.

Basie joined the Kansas-based Bennie Moten band in 1929. He soon became co-arranger with Eddie Durham and wrote "Moten Swing," an invaluable contribution to the development of swing music. Basie worked with the band for a number of years, alongside saxophonist Ben Webster, and for a period led the band himself under the name Count Basie and his Cherry Blossoms.

When the band folded in 1935, Basie formed a new band that featured tenor player Lester Young. It was around this time that Basie wrote "One O'Clock Jump" and his band started to get local radio airplay. At the end of 1936, Count Basie and His Barons of Rhythm moved from Kansas City to Chicago, where they honed their repertoire at the Grand Terrace Ballroom and undertook a recording session with producer John Hammond that formed Lester Young's first recordings.

Basie took his orchestra to New York in 1937. His first recordings for Decca followed, including "Pennies from Heaven" and "Honeysuckle Rose." In this period, Basie showcased some of the most notable blues singers of the era, such as Billie Holiday and Jimmy Rushing, who first appeared with the band at the Apollo Theater. Durham helped with arranging and composing, but for the most part the orchestra worked out its numbers in rehearsal, without notation, under Basie's guidance.

In early 1938, the Savoy hosted a "battle of the bands" between Basie and Chick Webb's group. Basie had Holiday, while Webb countered with Ella Fitzgerald. Afterward, *Metronome* magazine proclaimed "Basie's Brilliant Band Conquers Chick's." The publicity gave the Basie band wider recognition. Soon after, Benny Goodman recorded their signature tune, "One O'Clock Jump."

A few months later, Basie's band began playing at the Famous Door, which had a CBS network feed, giving them huge exposure. In 1939, Basie and his band made a major cross-country tour, including their first West Coast dates. In 1942, the band returned to the West Coast and appeared in the musical film *Reveille with Beverly* and a command performance for Armed Forces Radio, featuring Hollywood stars such as Clark Gable and Bette Davis. Other film appearances soon followed.

Through the early 1940s, the band continued to record on Okeh and Columbia. After the war, and with the rise of bebop, Basie temporarily disbanded the group, performing in smaller combos for a while, before reforming his group as a 16-piece orchestra in 1952. Soon after, Norman Granz got the new band into Birdland and promoted them through recordings on Mercury, Clef, and Verve. Basie's band shared the stage with bebop greats Charlie Parker, Dizzy Gillespie, and Miles Davis, and Basie began to embrace elements of the new style. Soon, his band was touring and recording again, with *Down Beat* reporting: "(Basie) has managed to assemble an ensemble that can thrill both the listener who remembers 1938 and the youngster who has never before heard a big band like this."

In the mid-1950s, by which time Neil Hefti was onboard as arranger, Basie's band was consistently backing the most prominent soloists in jazz, including Sarah Vaughan, Erroll Garner, George Shearing, and Stan Getz. In 1957, Basie released the live album *Count Basie at Newport*; "April in Paris" became a best-selling instrumental. In 1958, the band made its first European tour, and in 1959 Basie's band recorded a "greatest hits" double album, *The Count Basie Story*. They also teamed up with Billy Eckstine and arranger Quincy Jones for *Basie and Eckstine, Inc.*

Later that year, Basie appeared on television for a Fred Astaire dance feature on "Sweet Georgia Brown," followed in January 1960 by a performance at one of John F. Kennedy's inaugural balls. That summer, Basie and Duke Ellington combined to record *First Time! The Count Meets the Duke.*

For the rest of the 1960 and 1970s, Basie and his band remained busy with tours, recordings, and television and film appearances, most notably *Blazing Saddles* (1974). After a glittering career, Basie died in Hollywood, Florida on April 26, 1984 at the age of 79.

How to Play It

"Red Bank Boogie (G.I. Stomp)" is an original by Basie, named after his hometown. There are many recordings of it by Count Basie and His Orchestra, including this from 1938, featured on the compilation *The Count Basie Story*.

"Red Bank Boogie" finds Basie reveling in a mixture of typical boogie-woogie and blues riffs and licks. The lines in the first chorus – a mixture of simple arpeggios, pentatonics, and bluesy passing notes – reveal a tight, snappy, percussive swing style set against big tenth chords in the left-hand comping. The right-hand boogie riff in the second chorus is much more legato, an effect difficult to achieve between such fast-moving chords and with the jumps in hand position required. In this section, the left hand drops down to a simple root-fifth walking bass pattern with the odd passing note.

The final chorus, after the second exchange with the big band, shows Basie's mastery of the classic alternating octave boogie-woogie bass line set against idiomatic rhythmic chord stabs.

Vital Stats

Pianist: Count Basie

Song: "Red Bank Boogie (G.I. Stomp)"

Album: *The Count Basie Story* (compilation, rec. 1938)

Age at time of recording: 34

Transcr. Huw White

0:09

Up-tempo Boogie Swing ($\quarternote = 200$)

Chorus 1

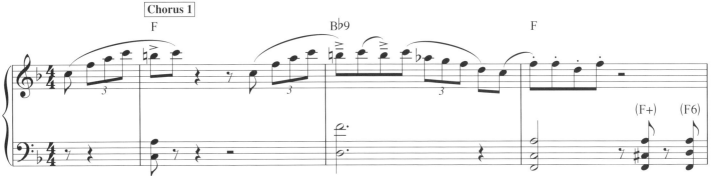

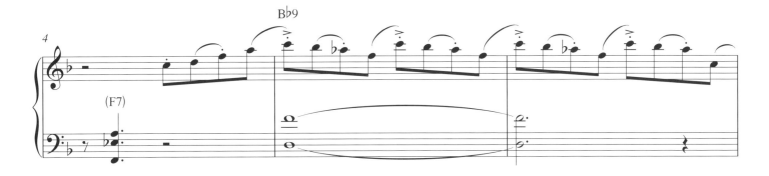

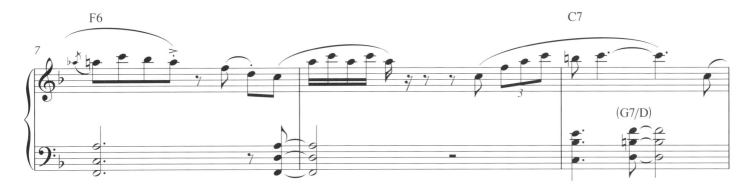

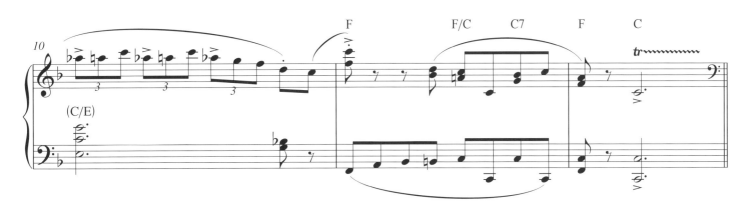

By Count Basie and Buck Clayton
© 1943 (Renewed) WB MUSIC CORP.
This arrangement © 2016 WB MUSIC CORP.
All Rights Reserved   Used by Permission

Red Bank Boogie (G.I. Stomp)

Chorus 4

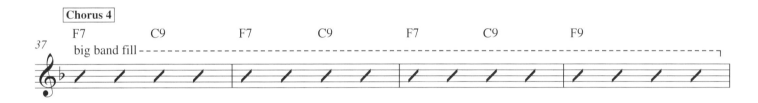

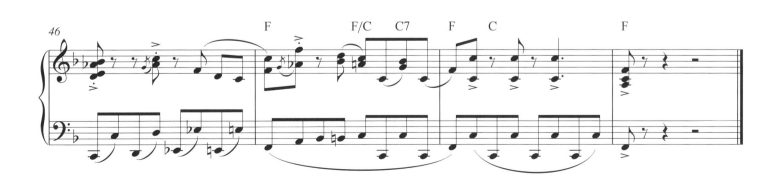

Erroll Garner

Erroll Garner was best known for his laid-back swinging style and his mastery of the ballad. His composition "Misty" is one of the most popular jazz standards of all time, and was famously featured in Clint Eastwood's 1971 film *Play Misty for Me*. With his charming stage presence, showmanship, and distinctive and impeccable musical taste, throughout his career Garner was able to bridge the gap between jazz in the nightclub and jazz in the concert hall.

Born on June 15, 1921 in Pittsburgh, Pennsylvania, Erroll Louis Garner began playing piano at just three years old. He attended the same high school as fellow pianists Billy Strayhorn and Ahmad Jamal. At the age of seven, he began performing on local radio and by the age of 11 was already gigging.

Garner was self-taught and, with an incredible ear, never learned to read music. In later life, he recorded his musical ideas on tape to be transcribed by others because he could not write them down. His inability to read music led to him gaining a superb musical memory. In one famous anecdote, after attending a concert by Russian classical pianist Emil Gilels, Garner was able to replicate large sections of the performance entirely by memory.

At age 23, Garner moved to New York, where he briefly worked with bassist Slam Stewart. Garner's first recordings were made in late 1944 and were subsequently issued as the five-volume

William P. Gottlieb collection / Library of Congress

Erroll Garner

"Everyday when I sit down to play, I learn something new."
–Erroll Garner

Overture to Dawn series on Blue Note Records. Although considered more of a swing player than a bop player, Garner famously recorded with Charlie Parker in 1947 on the *Cool Blues* session.

The majority of Garner's ensuing recorded work is in a trio setting, occasionally expanded to add Latin percussion. Garner's recording career advanced steadily through the late 1940s

into the 1950s with several successful sides such as "Fine and Dandy" and "Sweet 'n' Lovely." His live album *Concert by the Sea* (1955), featuring bassist Eddie Calhoun and drummer Denzil Best, was a top-seller of the day.

In 1963, Garner recorded with a full orchestra on *A New Kind of Love*, and in 1964 appeared in the U.K. on the music series *Jazz 625*, broadcast on the BBC's new second channel. He was known to be *The Tonight Show* host Johnny Carson's favorite jazz musician, giving many performances on Carson's show over the years.

Erroll Garner continued to record and perform throughout the 1960s and early 1970s, until his death on January 2, 1977, at the age of 55.

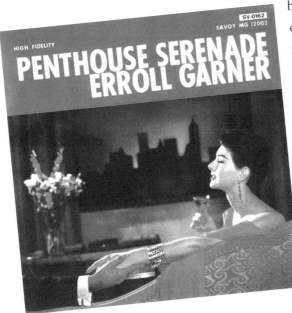

How to Play It

"Penthouse Serenade (When We're Alone)" is a popular song written by Will Jason and Val Burton in 1931. Erroll Garner performed it on his 1949 album *Penthouse Serenade.*

Erroll Garner was an undisputed master of the ballad and the right-hand block-chord approach, with an orchestral style of playing straight from the swing and stride eras, but an awareness of bop sensibilities. Garner was also known for his incredibly laid-back swinging style that stretched the beat at every opportunity.

All of these virtues are on display on "Penthouse Serenade," which after a double-handed block-chord intro, presents Garner sounding effortlessly relaxed as he accomplishes

a feat of right-hand chordal agility for the entire song, accompanied by a gently chugging left-hand stride.

Other idiomatic nuances include the octave half-step slides into many of the right-hand chords, the occasional tremolo and spread chord, and the rhythmic push and pull of phrases as Garner stretches the time in his right hand against an unwavering left.

Vital Stats

Pianist: Erroll Garner

Song: "Penthouse Serenade (When We're Alone)"

Album: *Penthouse Serenade* (1949)

Age at time of recording: 28

Penthouse Serenade (When We're Alone)

Transcr. Huw White

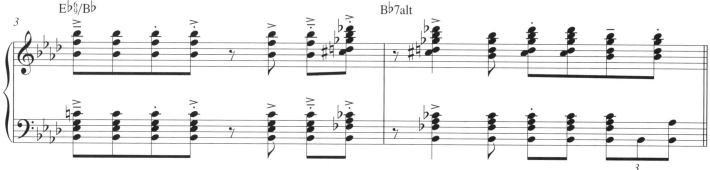

Bud Powell

"Bud is a genius."
–Charlie Parker

Bud Powell was one of the leading figures in the development of bebop, and his virtuosity in the style led many to call him the Charlie Parker of the piano. Powell was also a composer whose work helped extend the practiced range of jazz harmony.

Earl Rudolph "Bud" Powell (September 27, 1924 – July 31, 1966) was born and raised in Harlem, New York City. The son of a stride pianist, Powell took to his father's instrument and started to learn classical piano at age five. By age ten, he was assimilating the style of Fats Waller and James P. Johnson. A few years later, he began to try and match Art Tatum.

Around 1942, Powell met Thelonious Monk, who introduced him to the emerging circle of bebop musicians forming at Minton's Playhouse, where Monk was a resident. Monk treated Powell as his protégé, famously dedicating his composition "In Walked Bud" to him.

In the early 1940s, Powell played and recorded in dance orchestras, including that of Cootie Williams, with whom he made the first recording of Monk's "'Round Midnight." By the mid-1940s, Powell was in demand by various small-group leaders for Manhattan nightclub engagements. In 1945–46, he recorded with Dexter Gordon, J. J. Johnson, Sonny

Bud Powell

Stitt, Fats Navarro, and Kenny Clarke, among others, and became renowned for his ability to play at fast tempos, showing the strong influence of modern horn soloists such as Charlie Parker. In May 1947, Powell's career took a leap forward when Parker booked him as pianist for a quintet recording alongside Miles Davis, Tommy Potter, and Max Roach.

Although Powell struggled greatly with mental illness, resulting in hospitalization in 1947–48, it is generally agreed that he made his best recordings between 1949 and 1953. For his first Blue Note session, in August 1949, Powell was joined by Fats Navarro, Sonny Rollins, Tommy Potter, and Roy Haynes. The second session in 1951, a trio with Curley Russell and Max

Roach, was added by literary critic Harold Bloom to his short list of the greatest works of 20th-century American art.

The Amazing Bud Powell was recorded and released over a ten-year period from 1949–59, in five volumes on Blue Note. Volume 2, from which the transcription of Bud's solo on "I Want to Be Happy" is derived, was recorded in 1953 (released 1954) and features bassist George Duvivier and drummer Art Taylor. Powell also recorded over a dozen solo or trio sessions for Norman Granz in this period, with a variety of bassists and drummers, including Ray Brown, Percy Heath, Art Blakey, Kenny Clarke, Buddy Rich, and Art Taylor.

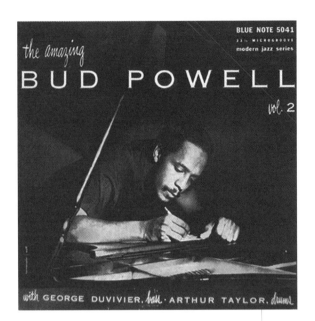

In the late 1950s, Powell's mental illness, exacerbated by the death of his brother Richie in a 1956 car crash, began to take its toll on his playing. However three albums for Blue Note in the late '50s showcased Powell's compositional skill.

Powell moved to Paris in 1959 and continued to perform and record, including a 1960 live recording from the Essen jazz festival with Clarke, Oscar Pettiford, and Coleman Hawkins. In December 1961, Powell recorded two albums for Columbia: *A Portrait of Thelonious* and *A Tribute to Cannonball*. Both albums were released posthumously. Powell appeared a final time on Blue Note in 1963, on Dexter Gordon's Our *Man in Paris*.

In 1964, Powell went back to New York for a return engagement at Birdland, accompanied by drummer Horace Arnold and bassist John Ore. Arnold called the honor of playing with the legendary Powell "the ultimate performance experience of my life."

Powell died in New York on July 31, 1966, at the age of just 41, after complications brought about by his mental health disorder. Several thousand people came out to pay their respects to a true genius of jazz at his Harlem funeral procession.

How to Play It

"I Want to Be Happy" was written by Vincent Youmans and Irving Caesar for the 1925 musical *No, No, Nanette*. The song was quickly adopted as a jazz standard. Bud Powell recorded it for his 1954 Blue Note album *The Amazing Bud Powell, Vol. 2*, with a trio featuring bassist George Duvivier and drummer Art Taylor.

Powell's solo on "I Want to Be Happy" shows him in the kind of fearless, creatively striving form he is best known for. Powell is generally acknowledged to be the first pianist to take the emerging bebop language of horn players, particularly that of Charlie Parker, and apply it to the piano. We can hear that in action here.

His right-hand melodic lines are interwoven with chromatic bop runs, encirculations, ornaments, and arpeggio figures, all executed with the attack of a hard-blown horn and an insistent, intensely driving swing feel. The fast tempo doesn't prevent Powell striving to explore upper harmonic extensions in a tirade of eighth notes and triplets, punctuated by largely bare left-hand voicings of root plus third or seventh, leaving the right hand free for unhindered harmonic adventurousness.

Vital Stats

Pianist: Bud Powell

Song: "I Want to Be Happy"

Album: *The Amazing Bud Powell, Vol. 2* (1954)

Age at time of recording: 30

Transcr. Huw White

I Want to Be Happy

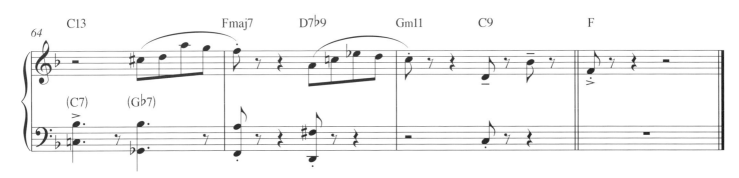

Ahmad Jamal

© Lewton Cole / Alamy Stock Photo

Ahmad Jamal

"I was never the practitioner in the sense of 12 hours a day, but I always thought about music. I think about music all the time"

–Ahmad Jamal

Over a career spanning seven decades, Ahmad Jamal has been heralded as one of the great jazz innovators, and as one of the leading pioneers of the "cool jazz" movement, which favored the use of space and time over the speed and freneticism of bebop.

Ahmad Jamal (né Frederick Russell Jones) was born on July 2, 1930 in Pittsburgh, Pennsylvania. At just three old he began imitating the piano playing of his uncle, before beginning formal piano lessons at age seven. Growing up, Jamal was surrounded by the influence of

Pittsburgh jazz greats such as Earl Hines, Billy Strayhorn, and Erroll Garner. By the age of 14 he was playing professional gigs himself, and was soon pointed out as a "coming great" by legendary pianist Art Tatum.

After graduating from High School in 1948, Jamal toured briefly with both George Hudson's Orchestra and his own band The Four Strings before moving to Chicago in 1950 (where he changed his name to Ahmad Jamal). While there, Jamal played an extended engagement at the Chicago Blue Note with his new smaller outfit The Three Strings, but his break came soon after when he was spotted performing with the group in New York City by record producer John Hammond.

Hammond, who also discovered the likes of Benny Goodman, Billie Holiday, and Count Basie, signed The Three Strings (later known as the Ahmad Jamal Trio) to the Okeh label, and they released their first record, *Ahmad's Blues*, in 1951. The trio featured guitarist Ray Crawford and bassists Eddie Calhoun (1950–52), Richard Davis (1953–54), and Israel Crosby (from 1954), and went on to record for Parrot (1953–55) and Epic (1955).

In 1957, the sound of Jamal's trio changed significantly when guitarist Crawford was replaced with drummer Vernel Fournier. The new trio's live album *But Not for Me* attracted huge interest in the jazz world, particularly for Jamal's trademark minimalist approach and extended vamps. The album remained on the Ten Best-selling charts for nearly two years.

After moving to New York in 1962 and taking a long break from his music career, Jamal resumed touring and recording in

1964 with bassist Jamil Nasser and made a new album, *Extensions* (1965). Jamal and Nasser worked together from 1964 to 1972, joined by drummer Frank Gant (1966–76), among others.

From 1970 onward Jamal began to explore the electric piano, frequently performing and recording using a Fender Rhodes, and releasing albums almost annually through to the millennium. Jamal has continued to explore primarily the jazz trio format through to the present day. Now in his eighties, Jamal still tours

and records. His most recent releases include *Saturday Morning* (2013) and the CD/DVD *Ahmad Jamal featuring Yusef Lateef Live at L'Olympia*, (2014). In 2011, Jamal was inducted into *Downbeat* magazine's Hall of Fame.

How to Play It

"All of You" is a popular song written by Cole Porter, published in 1954. Jamal performed it on his 1955 trio album *Chamber Music of the New Jazz*, released on Argo.

Jamal entered the jazz scene at a time when the speed and virtuosic improvisation inherent to bebop were key to the success of jazz musicians as artists. Jamal, however, took steps in the direction of a new movement, later coined "cool jazz." In contrast to bebop, cool jazz emphasized space and time, so be sure to relax and sit back on the beat.

Jamal used the piano like an orchestra, employing tension and release texturally as well as harmonically to create a level of surprise and variation in mood that might normally be expected of a big band. Be sure to listen closely to Jamal's performance, imitating how he brings out the drama, with dynamics and articulations frequently juxtaposed.

Vital Stats

Pianist: Ahmad Jamal

Song: "All of You"

Album: *Chamber Music of the New Jazz* (1955)

Age at time of recording: 24

0:58

Transcr. Huw White

Medium Swing (♩=140)

Chorus 1

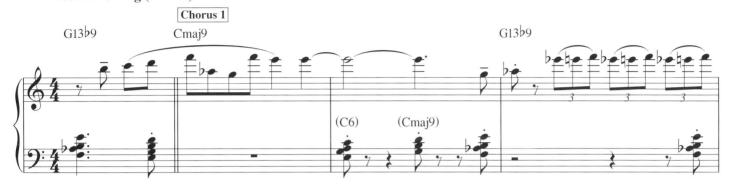

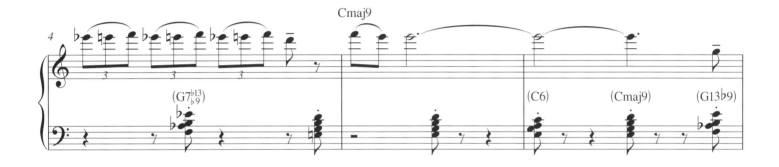

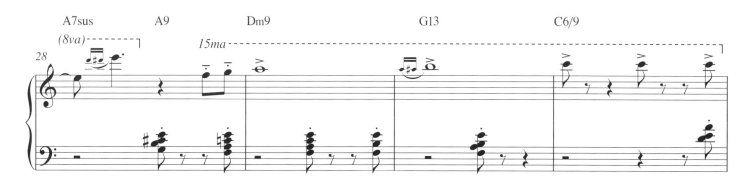

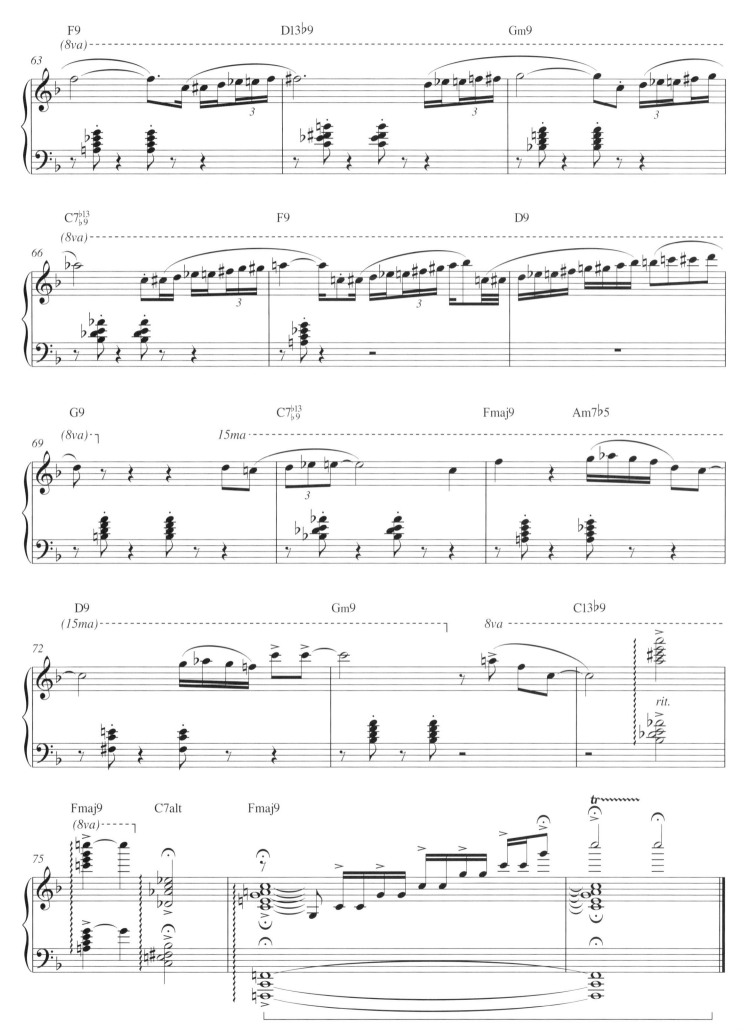

Lennie Tristano

"You could make your fingers reproduce exactly what you felt, if you really worked at it."

–Lennie Tristano

William P. Gottlieb collection / Library of Congress

Lennie Tristano

Many believe Lennie Tristano to be a true musical pioneer, one whose innovations were so far ahead of their time that his impact on the development of jazz, and the crucial link he provided between late 1940s bebop and late 1950s post-bop, were only truly appreciated later. Although Tristano was *Metronome*'s musician of the year in 1947, much of his public acknowledgment came further down the line. Tristano was elected to *Downbeat*'s Hall of Fame in 1979, and in 2013 was inducted into the Grammy Hall of Fame for his 1949 recording *Crosscurrents*. Tristano's teaching methods and methodical musical thinking helped to establish jazz as an academic art form, setting a precedent for the kind of jazz pedagogy that now flourishes in music conservatoires all over the world.

Leonard "Lennie" Joseph Tristano was born in Chicago on March 19, 1919. He began playing the family's pianola when he was just two or three years old, and started classical piano lessons when he was eight, only to indicate later that they had hindered his musical development.

Born with a severe visual impairment, by the age of ten Tristano was totally blind. Educated at the Illinois School for the Blind in Jacksonville, he learned several instruments – including piano, saxophones, trumpet, guitar, and drums – but his first gigs were on clarinet, at the age of 11. Early on he was influenced by pianists Bud Powell and Art Tatum, but as a natural innovator, Tristano soon preferred to seek his own style and approach to music.

Tristano studied music performance at the American Conservatory of Music in Chicago from 1938 until 1943. In the early 1940s, Tristano played tenor saxophone and piano for a variety of engagements, while giving private music lessons, including to saxophonist Lee Konitz. From 1943, Tristano also taught at the Axel Christensen School of Popular Music.

Tristano began to receive press coverage for his piano playing in 1944, appearing in *Metronome*'s summary of music in Chicago that year, and in *Downbeat* from 1945. In 1946, after a brief stay on Long Island, Tristano moved permanently to New York City to pursue a career as a jazz pianist. In 1947, he met Charlie Parker, who admired the pianist's originality. Before long, Tristano found himself playing in clubs and radio broadcasts alongside Bird and other bebop stars such as Dizzy Gillespie and Max Roach.

In 1948, Tristano played less often in clubs. After forming a quintet with Konitz, he began recording for the New Jazz label, which later became Prestige Records. Later that year, Tristano added one of his students to the group, saxophonist Warne Marsh.

Tristano's band recorded two pioneering sessions in 1949 featuring extremely linear, but unbebop-like, compositions. These were based on the harmonies of

existing jazz standards, as well as the very first free group improvisations – "Intuition" and "Digression." Soon after, the sextet played at the opening night of Birdland, "A Journey Through Jazz," followed by a five-week engagement at the club and appearances at other venues in the northeastern United States. With occasional personnel changes, Tristano's band continued performing into 1952, when Konitz left to join Stan Kenton's band, breaking up the core of the unit.

In 1953, Tristano made another highly innovative recording, *Descent into the Maelstrom*. A musical portrayal of an Edgar Allan Poe story of the same name, the album contained a mixture of solo and trio creations that used multi-tracking and had no preconceived harmonic structure, being based instead on motivic development.

Lennie Tristano recorded his first album for Atlantic Records in 1955. The eponymous album included solo and trio tracks that contained further experiments with tape-speed and multi-tracking, such as "Requiem," a tribute to the recently deceased Charlie Parker.

In the mid-1950s, Tristano began to focus his energy on music education.

As such, he became less active on the New York scene, but from 1958 still had occasional engagements at New York's Half Note Club. Tristano's second album for Atlantic was recorded in 1961. *The New Tristano* consisted entirely of piano solos, with no tape manipulation. Further solo recordings Tristano made the same year were released in the 1970s.

In 1964, Tristano re-formed his quintet with Konitz and Marsh for a short while, and in 1965 conducted a solo tour of Europe. His last public performance in the U.S. was in 1968, after which he decided to dedicate the remainder of his life to music education. Lennie Tristano died of a heart attack on November 18, 1978, at the age of 59.

How to Play It

"All The Things You Are" was written by Jerome Kern and Oscar Hammerstein for the 1939 musical *Very Warm for May*. It appears on Tristano's 1956 Atlantic album *Lennie Tristano*, with Lee Konitz on alto saxophone, Gene Ramey on bass, and Art Taylor on drums.

Lennie Tristano's solo on "All the Things You Are" demonstrates his linear approach, set against a harmonic chord bed in the left-hand voicing. Tristano's lines, predominantly uninterrupted eighth-note runs, are all about outlining the song harmony or whatever superimposed harmony connected to the original he wishes to imply at any moment.

The very first entry outlines a Bm7 chord which, supported by the left-hand voicing, works as a descending chromatic approach to the B♭m7 chord belonging to the original song harmony that appears a bar later. In bar 41, we see a portion of a descending D pentatonic scale immediately followed by the mirror image (only a half step lower) of the same portion of the Db pentatonic scale, ascending. These kinds of harmonic approaches and side-slips within the melodic line are typical of Tristano, and were extremely influential on future generations of pianists.

Tristano is also a master of rhythmic displacement of the melody, and of creating various cross-rhythms through melodic groupings and the subtle placement of accents within his lines. Bars 34–36 and 47–50 are good examples of this. This device had a clear influence on the playing style of Bill Evans, among others.

Vital Stats

Pianist: Lennie Tristano
Song: "All the Things You Are"
Album: *Lennie Tristano* (1956)
Age at time of recording: 36

Transcr. Huw White

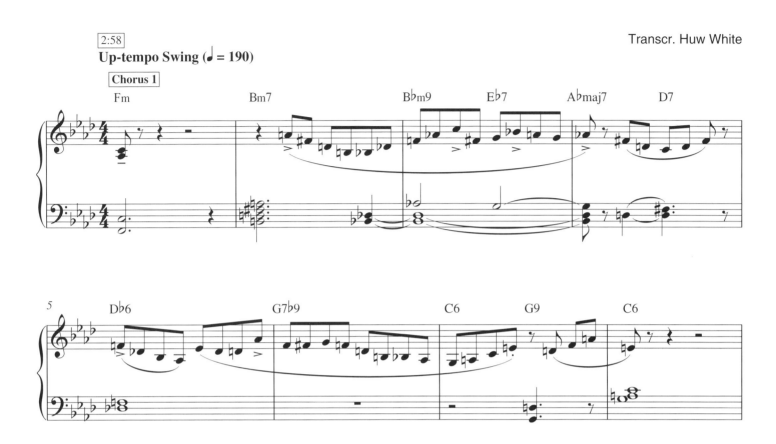

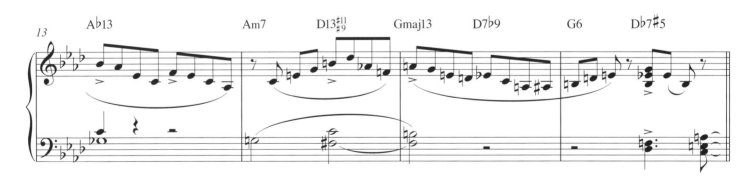

Lyrics by Oscar Hammerstein II
Music by Jerome Kern

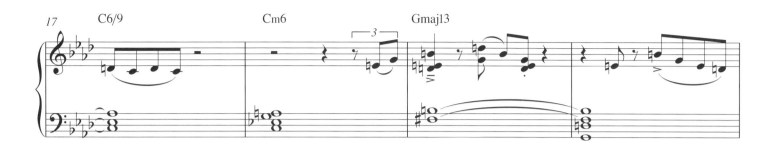

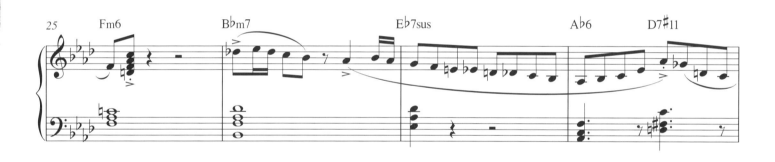

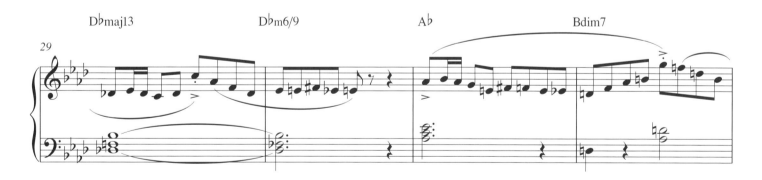

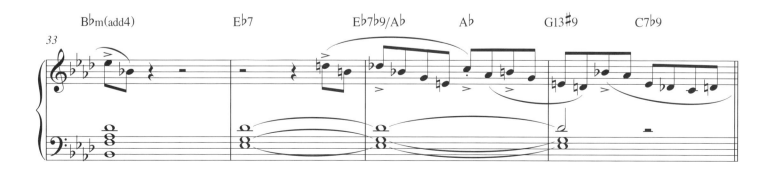

All the Things You Are

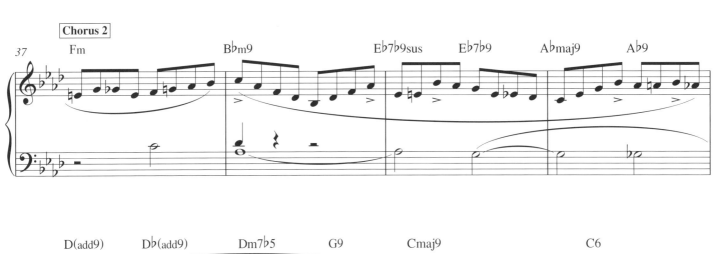

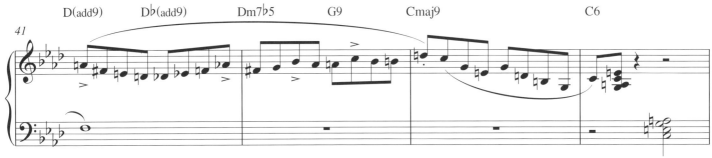

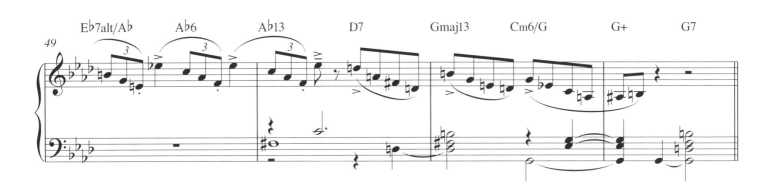

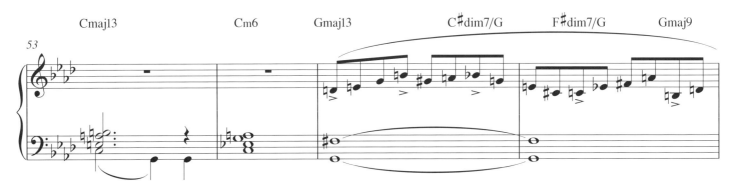

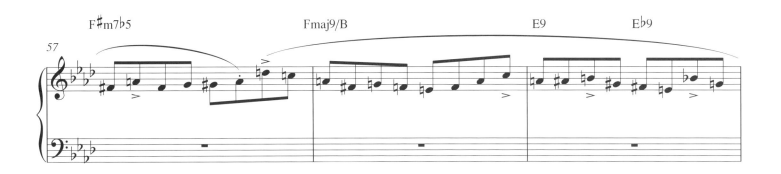

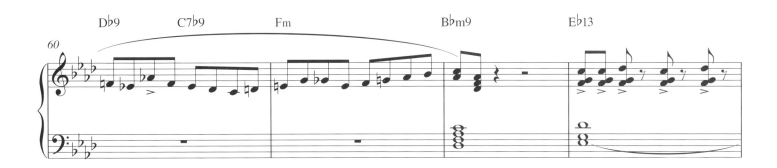

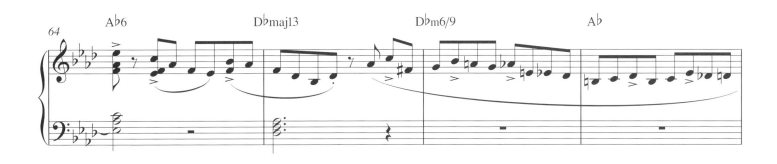

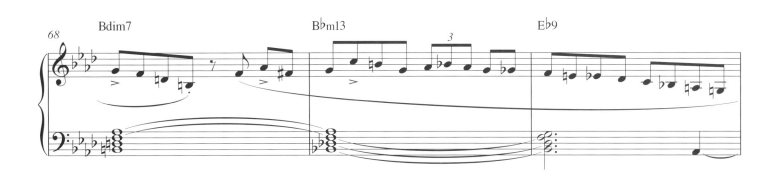

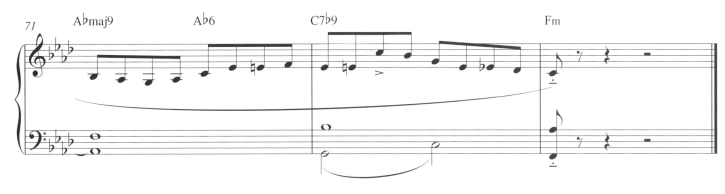

Hank Jones

Courtesy Photofest

Hank Jones

"I am the sum total of everything I have experienced musically."

–Hank Jones

Hank Jones had one of the longest and most remarkable careers in jazz, stretching over nearly eight decades – from the swing era and the birth of bebop into the 21st century. In that time, he recorded over 60 albums as a leader, and countless others as a sideman. He received the Grammy Award for Lifetime Achievement in 2009, in recognition of his accomplishments.

Born in Vicksburg, Mississippi on July 31, 1918, but growing up in Michigan, Henry "Hank" Jones was raised in a prodigiously musical family. His two younger brothers, trumpeter Thad and drummer Elvin, also became prominent jazz musicians. Elvin Jones was a founding member of John Coltrane's Classic Quartet.

Jones studied piano at an early age and came under the influence of stride pianists Earl Hines, Fats Waller, Teddy Wilson, and Art Tatum. By his early teens, Jones was performing locally in Michigan and Ohio.

In 1944, Jones met Lucky Thompson, who invited him to work at the Onyx Club in New York City. There, Jones was inspired by the scene's newly developing bebop style, and began exploring the music with musicians like Coleman Hawkins and Billy Eckstine. In autumn 1947, he began touring with Norman Granz's Jazz at the Philharmonic band. However, it was during his tenure as accompanist for legendary vocalist Ella Fitzgerald (1948–1953) that he truly blossomed and developed his highly sophisticated sense of harmony. During this period, he also made several historically important recordings with Charlie Parker, which included "The Song Is You," from *Now's the Time*,

recorded in December 1952, with Teddy Kotick on bass and Max Roach on drums.

Engagements with Artie Shaw and Benny Goodman followed, and recordings with artists such as Lester Young, Cannonball Adderley, and Wes Montgomery. For a time, Jones was house pianist on the Savoy label, and from 1959 through 1975 Jones was staff pianist for CBS studios; this led to him backing guests such as Frank Sinatra on *The Ed Sullivan Show*. Most famously, he played the piano accompaniment for Marilyn Monroe as she sang "Happy Birthday, Mr. President" to John F. Kennedy on May 19, 1962.

By the late 1970s, Jones's involvement as pianist and conductor with the Broadway musical *Ain't Misbehavin'* (based on the music of Fats Waller) had informed a wider audience of his musical talents. He recorded prolifically during the late 1970s and the 1980s, as an unaccompanied soloist, in duos with other pianists, including John Lewis and

Tommy Flanagan, and with various small ensembles, most notably the Great Jazz Trio. The group took this name in 1976, by which time Jones had already begun working at the Village Vanguard with its original members, Ron Carter and Tony Williams. It was Buster Williams rather than Carter, however, who took part in the trio's first recording session in 1976. By 1980, Jones's sidemen were Eddie Gómez and Al Foster, and Jimmy Cobb replaced Foster in 1982. The trio recorded with a number of all-star personnel, such as Art Farmer, Benny Golson, and Nancy Wilson.

Hank Jones continued to play, record, and tour at the highest level right up until his death. In the early 1980s, Jones toured Japan, where he performed and recorded with George Duvivier and Sonny Stitt. In 1995, he recorded a duo album of spirituals, hymns, and folksongs with Charlie Haden called *Steal Away*.

Into the 21st century, Jones was part of tenor saxophonist Joe Lovano's quartet, with bassist George Mraz and drummer Paul Motion, that recorded *Joyous Encounter* (2005). Jones also accompanied Diana Krall for "Dream a Little Dream of Me" on the album compilation *We All Love Ella* (2007). After one of the most remarkable lives, careers, and legacies in jazz, and a Grammy for Lifetime Achievement in 2009, Hank Jones died in New York on May 16, 2010. He was 91 years old.

How to Play It

"Have You Met Miss Jones?" was a popular song written by Rodgers and Hart that was first published in 1937. This recording is from a session around 1956 that appears on the compilation *Hank Jones: Complete Original Trio Recordings* (1953–61).

Jones's solo is typically graceful and elegant. His delicately swinging linear melodies are largely comprised of impeccably tasteful bebop and pentatonic runs that perfectly outline the chord changes, while the left hand is sparse and understated, offering subtle rhythmic and harmonic support. Jones only occasionally uses octaves in the right hand or more marked accents to draw attention to certain notes or phrases.

Jones manages to say a lot in this solo full of rich melodic language, while never giving the sense that he is overplaying. Notice how he gives each unique phrase a life of its own, simply through short, subtly placed breathing spaces.

Vital Stats

Pianist: Hank Jones

Song: "Have You Met Miss Jones?"

Album: *Complete Original Trio Recordings* (compilation, rec. 1953–61)

Age at time of recording: 38

Have You Met Miss Jones?

Transcr. Huw White

0:40

Up-tempo Swing (♩ = 208)

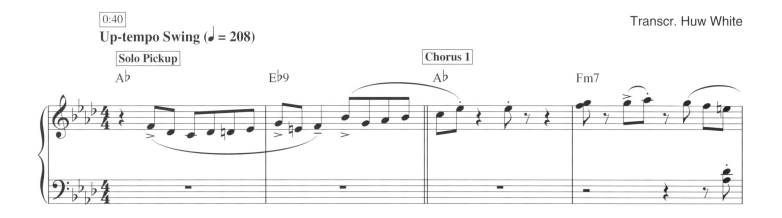

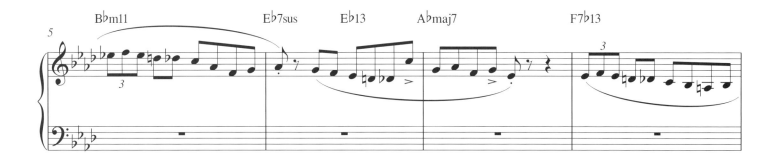

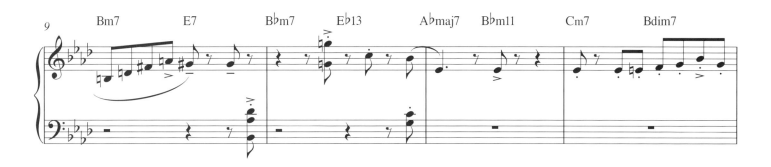

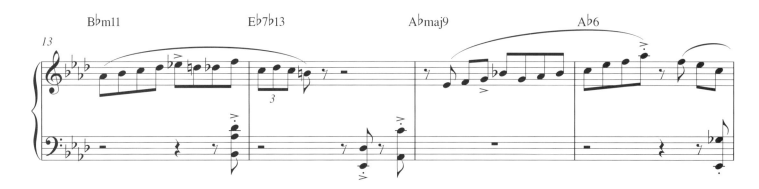

Art Tatum

Art Tatum is considered by many to be the greatest jazz pianist of all time. A true virtuoso, he reset the bar in the world of jazz piano with the technical brilliance of his performances, tossing down the gauntlet to an entire generation of aspiring pianists.

Arthur "Art" Tatum Jr. was born on October 13, 1909 in Toledo, Ohio to a guitarist father and a pianist mother, both of whom were church musicians. Blind from infancy, Tatum learned to play by ear, picking out church hymns by age three, learning tunes from the radio, and copying piano roll recordings his mother owned, developing an incredibly fast and accurate playing style in the process.

Tatum moved to the Columbus School for the Blind in 1925. He studied music and braille before returning to study classical piano at the Toledo School of Music. In 1927, Tatum began playing on a local Toledo radio station and soon had his own program. By age 19, Tatum was playing at local clubs, and as word of his incredible talent spread, national stars passing through Toledo such as Duke Ellington, Louis Armstrong, and Fletcher Henderson would go out of their way to hear him play.

In January 1932, vocalist Adelaide Hall, passing through Toledo on her world tour, discovered Tatum and employed him as her stage pianist. Hall returned to New York with Tatum later that year, introducing him to Harlem onstage at the Lafayette Theatre. A series of recordings with the pianist soon followed.

Tatum appeared at a 1933 "cutting contest" at Morgan's bar in New York City, against some of his own greatest

William P. Gottlieb collection / Library of Congress

Art Tatum

influences: stride pianists Fats Waller, James P. Johnson, and Willie "The Lion" Smith. In a historic debut that helped propel his meteoric rise to success, Tatum outplayed the elite competition, heralding the demise of the stride era. Tatum remained in New York for a few months, recording his first four solo sides on the Brunswick label in March 1933, before returning to Ohio and spending the mid-1930s performing around the American Midwest. Later in the decade, he spent more time playing and recording in both New York and

"Look, you come in here tomorrow, and anything you do with your right hand I'll do with my left"

–Art Tatum to Bud Powell

Los Angeles, and undertook a tour of England.

In 1941, Tatum recorded two well-received sessions for Decca Records with singer Big Joe Turner, and in 1943 won *Esquire* magazine's first jazz popularity poll. Inspired by Nat King Cole, Tatum formed his own jazz trio in 1943 with guitarist Tiny Grimes and bassist Slam Stewart, recording exclusively with the trio for almost two years. Tatum later recorded with other musicians, including a notable session with the 1944 Esquire Jazz All-Stars, which included Louis Armstrong, Billie Holiday, and other jazz greats – at the Metropolitan Opera House in New York City.

Although Tatum was universally admired, his popularity faded slightly with the birth of bebop in the mid-to-late 1940s. However, in the mid-1950s he recorded a number of group sessions for Norman Granz, with jazz greats such as Benny Carter, Roy Eldridge, Lionel Hampton, and Ben Webster. One of the final sessions of Tatum's life, a 1956 session with Webster, produced *The Art Tatum-Ben Webster Quartet*, from which the transcription of Tatum's solo on "Night and Day" is derived.

In the last two years of his life, Tatum regularly played at Baker's Keyboard Lounge in Detroit, including in his final public performance in April 1956. Art Tatum died on November 5, 1956 in Los Angeles after suffering kidney failure. He was just 47 years old, but in his short career he established himself as arguably the greatest jazz pianist of all time. In 1964, Art Tatum was posthumously inducted into the *Downbeat* Jazz Hall of Fame, and in 1989 was honoured with the Grammy Lifetime Achievement Award.

How to Play It

"Night and Day" was written by Cole Porter for the 1932 musical *Gay Divorce*. It soon became a staple of the Great American Songbook. Art Tatum recorded it for the 1956 Verve album *Art Tatum & Ben Webster Quartet*, which features Red Callender on bass and Bill Douglass on drums.

Never given to pianistic understatement, the virtuosic and exuberant Tatum comes tearing into this solo with torrents of triplet and 16th-note runs that demonstrate both his formidable technique and harmonic prowess. More than sitting on top of the beat, Tatum's subdivisions fire out with an explosive force that ensures the rhythm section keep with him and not vice versa.

Although the occasional rhythmic nuance or left-hand tenth chord gives away Tatum's stride heritage, this recording, toward the end of his life, shows how he was a pioneer of the kind of free-ranging melodic improvisation that is usually attributed to bebop trailblazers like Bud Powell. While still employing some of his signature runs, arpeggiated figures, and embellishments – such as the sweeping hand-crossing pattern finished with a left-hand top C that appears in bar 26 – there are also plenty of highly improvised, harmonically creative lines.

Vital Stats

Pianist: Art Tatum

Song: "Night and Day"

Album: *Art Tatum & Ben Webster Quartet* (1956)

Age at time of recording: 46

3:15

Transcr. Huw White

Medium Up-tempo Swing, "2 feel" ($\mathord{\downarrow} = 184$)

Bill Evans

"I want my work – and the trios if possible – to sing."
–Bill Evans

Bill Evans is considered by many to have been the most influential jazz pianist of the post-war era. His use of impressionist harmony, block chords, and immensely lyrical melodic lines continue to inspire jazz pianists today. Many of his compositions have become jazz standards, widely played and recorded. In his relatively short life and career, Evans received 31 Grammy nominations and seven awards, and was inducted into the *Downbeat* Jazz Hall of Fame.

Born in Plainfield, New Jersey on August 16, 1929, William John Evans began taking piano lessons around the age of five, taking up violin and flute soon after. Until his teens, Evans played only classical music, but during high school came under the influence of 20th-century composers such as Stravinsky and concepts such as bitonality and impressionism. Evans was also exposed to jazz for the first time, and began listening to pianists like Earl Hines, Bud Powell, George Shearing, and Nat King Cole.

In September 1946, Evans enrolled at Southeastern Louisiana University, where he studied classical piano. He graduated in 1950 after performing Beethoven's Piano Concerto No. 3 for his senior recital. Evans then spent the

© AF archive / Alamy Stock Photo

Bill Evans

summer on tour accompanying Billie Holliday in Herbie Fields' band. In 1951, Evans was drafted into the U.S. Army, and, after three years of service, took a year-long sabbatical in 1954 to work solely on his piano technique.

Evans moved to New York in 1955, where he worked with bandleader and influential theorist George Russell. By 1956, Evans had released his debut album *New Jazz Conceptions* (from which the transcription of his solo on "Five" is derived) and began appearing on albums by the likes of Charlie Mingus, Oliver Nelson, and Art Farmer.

In 1958, Evans joined Miles Davis's sextet, and in 1959, Evans's talents were flung into the limelight upon the release of *Kind of Blue*, which became the best-selling jazz album of all time. Later that year, Evans began his career as a leader. His first trio, featuring bassist Scott LaFaro and drummer Paul Motian, is now regarded as one of the seminal trios of modern jazz. In 1961, at the height of the trio's success, LaFaro died in a car accident. After months of seclusion, Evans re-emerged with a new trio, featuring bassist Chuck Israels.

Perhaps influenced by fellow pianist Lennie Tristano (whom Evans openly admired) in its incorporation of overdubbing techniques, Evans recorded *Conversations with Myself* in 1963, an original and innovative solo album that won Evans his first Grammy. After a quiet period, in 1966 Evans began a musical relationship with bassist Eddie Gómez that would last a decade, producing a string of successful trio albums with a number of different drummers, such as *Bill Evans at the Montreux Jazz Festival*, which featured Jack DeJohnette on drums, and won Evans a second Grammy. Further highlights from this period include *Bill Evans at Town Hall* (1966), a second duet album with guitarist Jim Hall called *Intermodulation* (1966), and the solo album *Alone* (1968) that won Evans his third Grammy award.

In 1970, Evans recorded *From Left to Right*, featuring his first use of electric piano. In 1971, Evans recorded an all-originals album, *The Bill Evans Album*, which featured Gómez and drummer Marty Morrell, and won two Grammy awards. Other notable albums included *The Tokyo Concert* (1973), *Since We Met* (1974), and *But Beautiful* (1974), featuring trio plus saxophonist Stan Getz in live performances from the Netherlands and Belgium. Evans also recorded two duet albums with singer Tony Bennett, *The Tony Bennett/Bill Evans Album* (1975) and *Together Again* (1977).

Two trio albums recorded in 1977, *I Will Say Goodbye* and *You Must Believe in Spring*, were Evans's last with Gómez. His final working trio was with Marc Johnson on bass and Joe LaBarbera on drums. In August 1979, Evans recorded his final studio album, *We Will Meet Again*, which went on to win another Grammy. Evans died on September 15, 1980 after a long battle with drug addiction. He was 51 years old.

How to Play It

Bill Evans's tune "Five" is the second track on his 1956 album *New Jazz Conceptions* (Riverside). Featuring Teddy Kotick on bass and Paul Motion on drums, for some time "Five" was Evans's encore tune.

"Five" is essentially a "rhythm changes," a 32-bar AABA form, split into four sections of eight measures, based on Gershwin's "I Got Rhythm." However, in typical Evans fashion, "Five" is thoroughly re-harmonized. Each chorus starts on an F♯ dominant chord and works around a chain of dominants through the Circle of Fifths back to the tonic B♭, giving Evans the opportunity to create a number of melodic sequences. These often feature rhythmic displacement, a preferred device of Evans; another tune on *New Jazz Conceptions* is even called "Displacement."

Of interest on this relatively early recording is that Evans – who is typically celebrated for his role in pioneering the rootless voicing – still employs bass notes in many of his left-hand voicings, in a manner not dissimilar to Bud Powell, one of his stated influences.

In terms of execution, as ever Evans's bebop style is bouncy and pushy, with his subtle eighth-note swing feel leaning toward a straighter approach at times. Note how he uses heavy accents to emphasize cross-rhythms, rhythmic displacement, and syncopation within his lines.

Vital Stats

Pianist: Bill Evans

Song: "Five"

Album: *New Jazz Conceptions* (1956)

Age at time of recording: 27

Transcr. Huw White

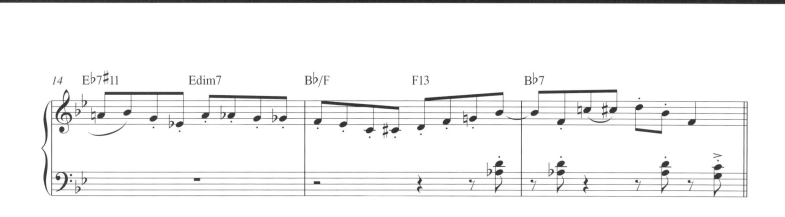

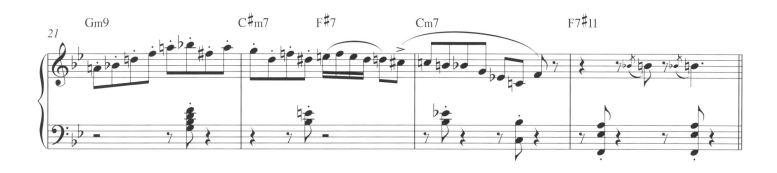

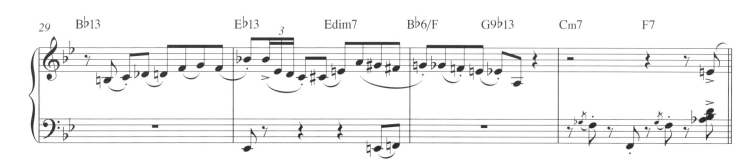

Red Garland

© Cecil Charles CTSImages

Red Garland

"Nobody had to tell me to practice because I was playing piano all day."
–Red Garland

began his musical studies on the clarinet and alto saxophone, but was a late starter to the piano, nearly 17 years old by the time he began playing. However, Garland spent copious amounts of time practicing and rapidly developed into a highly proficient player.

After the Second World War, Garland performed with Billy Eckstine, Roy Eldridge, Coleman Hawkins, Charlie Parker, and Lester Young. He found steady work in the cities of Boston, New York, and Philadelphia. In the late 1940s, he toured with Eddie Vinson – along with saxophonist John Coltrane. By this point, Garland was beginning to show signs of the influence of Ahmad Jamal and Charlie Parker's pianist Walter Bishop.

Garland rose to public attention in 1955 when he joined the Miles Davis Quintet featuring John Coltrane, Philly Joe Jones, and Paul Chambers and the group recorded their famous Prestige albums, *Miles: The New Miles Davis Quintet,* plus *Workin, Steamin', Cookin',* and *Relaxin'.* His style is prominent in these seminal recordings – evident in his distinctive chord voicings, sophisticated accompaniment, and musical references to Ahmad Jamal. Garland appeared on the first of Davis's many Columbia recordings, *'Round About Midnight* (1957). Soon afterward he left the band, but later returned to play on another of Davis's classic albums, *Milestones* (1958).

In 1958, Garland formed his own trio, initially with bassist Paul Chambers and drummer Art Taylor. With occasionally varying personnel the trio went on to record with Pepper Adams, Nat Adderley, Kenny Burrell, and Eddie "Lockjaw" Davis, among others. The trio also recorded as a quintet with John Coltrane and Donald Byrd.

Red Garland is best known for his highly influential work with the Miles Davis Quintet in the late 1950s. Garland's trademark block-chord technique, commonly assimilated and deployed by jazz pianists up to the present day, was truly original and unique. It differed from the methods of the technique's early pioneers George Shearing and Milt Buckner, particularly in the omission of the bass note in the left hand, which further led to a style of left-hand comping, the "rootless voicing," more frequently associated with future Davis bandmate Bill Evans.

William "Red" Garland was born in Dallas, Texas on May 13, 1923. He

Altogether, Garland led 19 recording sessions while at Prestige Records and 25 sessions for Fantasy Records. In his relatively short career in the public eye, Garland's highly distinctive style ensured that he would leave his influential mark on ensuing generations of jazz pianists. Although largely out of the limelight, Garland continued recording until his death in April 1984 at the age of 60.

How to Play It

"If I Were a Bell" was written by Frank Loesser for his 1950 musical *Guys and Dolls*. It has become a jazz standard since Miles Davis recorded it for his 1958 Prestige album *Relaxin' with the Miles Davis Quintet*, which features tenor saxophonist John Coltrane, bassist Paul Chambers, drummer Philly Joe Jones, and Garland on piano.

Garland's solo on "If I Were a Bell" perfectly encapsulates his style and qualities as a pianist. He produces a long string of bluesy bebop lines, decorated with tight triplet and 16th-note ornaments that perfectly outline the harmonic changes. His right-hand touch is effortlessly graceful and light, yet percussive and bright, with a groovy snappiness to his swing feel. His left-hand comping riffs away on the "and" of beats 2 and 4, a Garland trademark, with the kinds of left-hand rootless voicings that are generally associated with Bill Evans recordings of the period.

The block-chord sections, for which Garland is most known and imitated, show how the left hand remains generally static on a four-note rootless voicing per each chord change, beating out the same rhythm as the right-hand melody, which can be harmonized with anything from an open octave up to a five-note voicing, creating occasional bluesy dissonance against the left hand as it moves through passing chords.

Vital Stats

Pianist: Red Garland

Song: "If I Were a Bell"

Album: *Relaxin' with the Miles Davis Quintet* (1958)

Age at time of recording: 35

If I Were a Bell

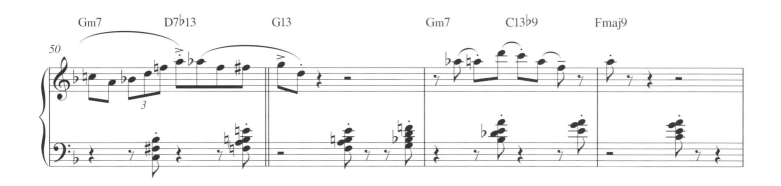

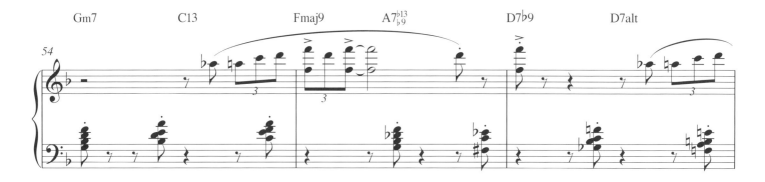

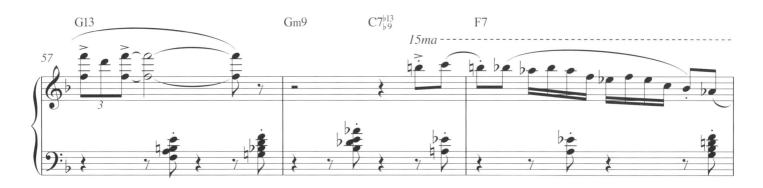

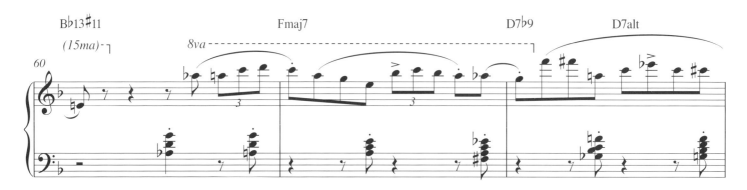

Sonny Clark

Sonny Clark

"Some people sound like they're trying to swing. Sonny just flows along naturally."
–Ira Gitler

In his short life and career, Sonny Clark burned fast and bright, releasing 11 albums as a leader (nine on Blue Note), and appearing as a sideman on nearly 50 others in a recording career that lasted just eight years, between 1954 and 1962. Clark's output as a sideman reflects the high regard in which he was held by his hard-bop era contemporaries. Such was Bill Evans's admiration for Clark, and sorrow at his premature passing, that he named a song for him – "N.Y.C.'s No Lark," an anagram of Sonny Clark's name.

Conrad Yeatis "Sonny" Clark was born on July 21, 1931 in Herminie, Pennsylvania, and raised at the Redwood Inn Hotel, which held popular weekend jazz dances. Clark started piano lessons at the age of four. By the age of six he was playing professionally at the hotel. He appeared on a radio show performing a boogie-woogie, which resulted in the *Pittsburgh Courier* publishing an article about the young prodigy.

With such early exposure to live jazz – and Art Tatum, Fats Waller, Count Basie, and Duke Ellington on the radio – Clark soon fell in love with the music he was surrounded by. At high school he took up bass and vibes, playing with the school band, while already performing professionally on piano around Pittsburgh. At the age of 15, Clark appeared alongside the likes of Earl Hines, Mary Lou Williams, Billy Strayhorn, Erroll Garner, Billy Eckstine, and Ray Brown on the bill for a historic "Night of the Stars" Concert at the Syria Mosque, which celebrated the music of Pittsburgh's jazz superstars.

© Ray Avery CTSImages

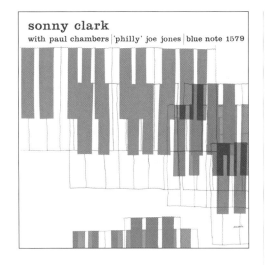

sonny clark
with paul chambers | 'philly' joe jones | blue note 1579

Visiting an aunt in California in 1951, the 20-year-old Clark decided to stay and began working with saxophonist Wardell Gray. In 1953, Clark went on to San Francisco with Oscar Pettiford and after a couple of months was working with clarinetist Buddy DeFranco. Clark toured the United States and Europe with DeFranco until January 1956, when he joined the Lighthouse All-Stars, led by bassist Howard Rumsey.

Clark relocated to New York City in 1957 and worked briefly as an accompanist for singer Dinah Washington. In New York, Clark's skill, particular in comping, quickly put him in high demand as a sideman among the hard-bop community. He began recording frequently for Blue Note Records, with artists such as Donald Byrd, Paul Chambers, John Coltrane, Dexter Gordon, Art Farmer, Philly Joe Jones, and Hank Mobley. He also recorded sessions with Charles Mingus, Sonny Rollins, Billie Holiday, Stanley Turrentine, and Lee Morgan.

In 1957, Clark recorded his first studio album as a leader on Blue Note, *Dial "S" for Sonny*. Two more albums followed that same year, *Sonny's Crib* and *Sonny Clark Trio*. The latter included the John Lewis tune "Two Bass Hit," from which the transcription of Clark's solo here is derived. *Sonny Clark Trio* featured bassist Paul Chambers and drummer Philly Joe Jones. Clark made a further six albums on Blue Note: *Sonny Clark Quintets* (1957), *Cool Struttin'* (1958), *The Art of The Trio* (1958), *Blues in the Night* (1958), *My Conception* (1959), and *Leapin' and Lopin'* (1961).

Clark struggled greatly with addiction to drugs and alcohol, and his career was tragically cut short when he died of a heart attack in New York City on January 13, 1963. He was just 31 years old, but left behind a firm imprint and influence on both the 1960s jazz scene and the ensuing generations of jazz musicians.

How to Play It

"Two Bass Hit" was a tune written by pianist John Lewis for Dizzy Gillespie's big band. Sonny Clark performed it on his 1958 Blue Note album *Sonny Clark Trio*, which features Paul Chambers on bass and Philly Joe Jones on drums.

"Two Bass Hit" demonstrates Sonny Clark's mastery of melodic bebop language, as he outlines the changes effortlessly, with plenty of horn-like ornaments and idiomatic encirculations.

Like many of the great bebop players, he is able to weave seamlessly between blues lines and running the changes. His left-hand approach is comparable to Bud Powell in its sparseness, both rhythmically and harmonically, leaving maximum room for the right hand to explore and carry the harmonic interest.

Clark's swing is bouncy and joyful, and his lines contain an expressive range of articulations – from heavy accents on the cornerstones of his phrases to almost ghosted passing notes – creating underlying cross-rhythms and a compelling sense of propulsion. In bars 13–15 Clark more intentionally sets up a cross rhythm, grouping his phrases in dotted-quarter notes across the meter of 4, and again in bars 48–52, this time grouping his phrases in beats of 3 across the meter of 4.

Clark's approach in general is playful, as he throws in a number of quotes, often at the top of choruses, including Monk's "Rhythm-a-Ning" (bar 61), which was first released a year before, in 1957.

Vital Stats

Pianist: Sonny Clark

Song: "Two Bass Hit"

Album: *Sonny Clark Trio* (1958)

Age at time of recording: 27

By Dizzy Gillespie and John Lewis
Copyright © 1948 (Renewed) Music Sales Corporation (ASCAP) and MJQ Music, Inc. (BMI)
This arrangement Copyright © 2016 Music Sales Corporation (ASCAP) and MJQ Music, Inc. (BMI)
All Rights for MJQ Music, Inc. Administered by Hal Leonard - Milwin Music Corp.
International Copyright Secured   All Rights Reserved
Reprinted by Permission

Two Bass Hit

Wynton Kelly

"It's happy sounding all the time. It's got a West Indian kind of hop to it. Always sparkling."

–Jimmy Cobb

Wynton Kelly is celebrated among musicians for his lively, boppy blues-based playing, and for his joyous, bouncy swing feel. Perhaps best known for his work with Miles Davis, and his appearance on *Kind of Blue*, from which the transcription of his solo on "Freddie Freeloader" is derived, he was also a master of the trio setting, and one of the finest accompanists in jazz.

Born in Brooklyn, New York on December 2, 1931 to Jamaican parents, Wynton Charles Kelly began playing the piano at the age of four. He attended the High School of Music and Art and the Metropolitan Vocational High School in New York, where he studied bass and theory.

From a young age, Kelly played organ in local churches and jammed with many contemporaries who went on to have careers in jazz. He started his professional career when he was just 11, learning to entertain audiences as part of R&B groups, touring the Caribbean

Wynton Kelly

as part of Ray Abrams's band when he was just 15. A year later, Kelly made his recording debut, playing on saxophonist Hal Singer's "Cornbread," which became a *Billboard* R&B chart-topping hit in 1948. Kelly also played in R&B bands with Hot Lips Page (1948),

Eddie "Cleanhead" Vinson (1949), and Eddie "Lockjaw" Davis (1950).

Blue Note released Kelly's debut as a jazz leader in 1951, a trio album called *Piano Interpretations*, which revealed the influence of Bud Powell and Teddy Wilson on his playing. Over the

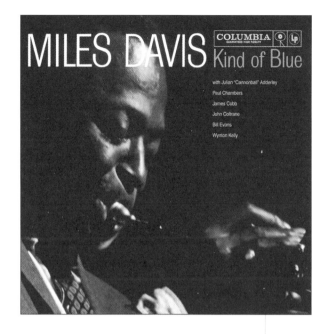

MILES DAVIS — COLUMBIA — Kind of Blue

with Julian "Cannonball" Adderley
Paul Chambers
James Cobb
John Coltrane
Bill Evans
Wynton Kelly

following year, Kelly's reputation grew as he played and recorded with bands led by Dinah Washington, Lester Young, and Dizzy Gillespie.

After two years' service in the military, which saw Kelly become musical director of a traveling show, he was reunited with Washington and Gillespie in 1954. He also began to work with Charles Mingus, and was adept at adjusting to both big and small band settings. From 1956 into the early 1960s, Kelly appeared on albums by most major jazz leaders of the period, including Billie Holiday, Sonny Rollins, Art Blakey, Julian "Cannonball" Adderley, Wes Montgomery, and countless others. In 1958, Kelly recorded his second album as leader, a quartet album called *Piano*.

Kelly joined Miles Davis's band in January 1959, staying with the trumpeter until March 1963. He appeared on the best-selling jazz album of all time, *Kind of Blue*, as well as *Someday My Prince Will Come* and a number of live albums. During this period, Kelly continued to record with different leaders, including with other members of the Davis band, such as saxophonist John Coltrane. In 1959, Kelly made his first album for Vee-Jay Records, *Kelly Great*, in a quintet containing Wayne Shorter.

After leaving Davis, Kelly performed, toured, and recorded with his own trio, which featured bassist Paul Chambers and drummer Jimmy Cobb. In May 1964, the calypso track "Little Tracy" from Kelly's first album for Verve, *Comin' in the Back Door*, reached No. 38 on *Billboard*'s R&B chart. The trio, often teaming up with other star front-line players, continued performing and recording until 1969, when Chambers died.

Kelly's final recording session was with saxophonist Dexter Gordon, in the autumn of 1970. Kelly died in Toronto, Canada on April 12, 1971 following an epileptic seizure. He was just 39 years old. Such was the level of respect for him within the jazz community that an all-star memorial concert in his honor was held on June 28.

How to Play It

"Freddie Freeloader" is a composition by Miles Davis that was the second track on the best-selling jazz album of all time, Davis's *Kind of Blue* (1959, Columbia).

Kelly's solo on "Freddie Freeloader" is typically swinging and full of the trademark bluesy licks, ornaments, melodic encirculations, and crushed notes so synonymous with his sound. Kelly's timing is relaxed but focused, particularly with his boppish 16th-note interjections that tend to be driving and on top of the beat. Listen to how Kelly achieves his bouncy right-hand style through the playful interplay of staccato, legato, and accented notes. His subtle use of space between statements, and casual hints of call and response and melodic sequence devices (e.g., bars 9–10 and 21–22) all help to give the music a natural sense of momentum.

The subtle yet ever-intentional rhythmic placement and articulation of his left-hand chords help to effortlessly frame and propel forward the work of his right hand, with both hands always working as a unit.

Vital Stats

Pianist: Wynton Kelly
Song: "Freddie Freeloader"
Album: *Kind of Blue* (1959)
Age at time of recording: 28

Freddie Freeloader

Transcr. Huw White

0:44

Medium Swing ($\bullet$ = 130)

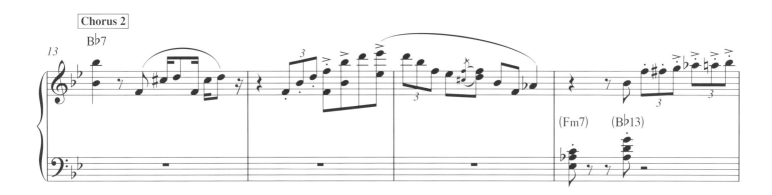

Tommy Flanagan

"I wasn't old enough to go in, but I could stand right by the side door. To have heard the records and then to hear what could be done in person was a great thing to me."
–Tommy Flanagan.

Tommy Flanagan

In his 45-year recording career, Tommy Flanagan recorded more than three dozen albums under his own name and more than 200 as a sideman. He appeared on many seminal albums with jazz greats such as Miles Davis, John Coltrane, Sonny Rollins, and Ella Fitzgerald, receiving five Grammy nominations along the way.

Thomas Lee Flanagan was born on March 16, 1930 in Detroit, Michigan. At the age of six he took up clarinet, but within a few years he preferred to play the household piano, taking lessons with Gladys Wade Dillard, who also taught Kirk Lightsey and Barry Harris. Flanagan graduated from Northern High School, which was attended by other future musicians, including Sonny Red. His early influences included Art Tatum, Teddy Wilson, and Nat King Cole, but he

and his friends soon grew more interested in modern bebop players such as Bud Powell, who would have a strong effect on Flanagan's improvisational style.

Flanagan played his first gig around the age of 14, with trombonist Frank Rosolino. As a teenager, he played alongside Pepper Adams and Kenny Burrell in a band led by Lucky Thompson

and sat in with Charlie Parker when he was in town. In 1949, at the age of 19, Flanagan had his first residency, at the Blue Bird Inn, Detroit. The following year, he played with Rudy Rutherford of the Count Basie band, and saxophonist George Benson in Toledo.

After two years' serving in the army, from 1951–1953, Flanagan returned to

Jan Persson CTSImages

Detroit and became pianist at the Blue Bird again, working with Burrell, Donald Byrd, and Yusef Lateef, among others.

In 1956, Flanagan moved to New York with Burrell and found work in clubs and studios, recording *Detroit-New York Junction* with Thad Jones in March that year. He also recorded sessions with Miles Davis and Sonny Rollins, most notably for Rollins's *Saxophone Colossus*. He also had his first stint accompanying Ella Fitzgerald. Later that year he joined trombonist J. J. Johnson, with whom he recorded several albums in 1957 and toured Europe. While in Sweden, Flanagan recorded his first album as a leader, *Overseas*, with bassist Wilbur Little and drummer Elvin Jones. Soon afterward, he had a short stint in Miles Davis's band.

Throughout the late 1950s and early 1960s Flanagan appeared on a number of groundbreaking albums, including the 1960 releases John Coltrane's *Giant Steps* and *The Incredible Jazz Guitar of Wes Montgomery*, from which the transcription of Flanagan's solo on "West Coast Blues" is derived. Between 1959 and 1962,

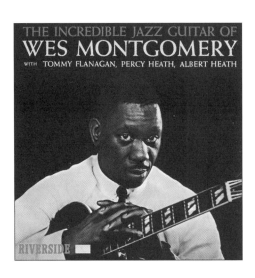

Flanagan worked with Harry Edison and Coleman Hawkins and recorded albums with a number of pre-bebop era musicians such as Lionel Hampton, Jo Jones, and Pee Wee Russell. He also had a trio in New York with guitarist Jim Hall and bassist Percy Heath.

From 1962, Flanagan was Ella Fitzgerald's full-time accompanist, touring internationally, until he joined Art Farmer's New York Jazz Sextet in 1965, which recorded *Group Therapy*. In 1966, Flanagan became Tony Bennett's accompanist. In 1968, Flanagan returned to Fitzgerald and her intense touring schedule, in the role of musical director. In 1975, after years refining his trio sound while opening up shows for the singer, Flanagan released his first record as a leader since 1960, *The Tommy Flanagan Tokyo Recital*. Flanagan ended his labor-intensive role with Fitzgerald in 1978, after suffering a heart attack.

Post Fitzgerald, Flanagan primarily focused on performing as a leader, usually in a trio setting. In 1979, Flanagan was a guest on the first series of Marian McPartland's *Piano Jazz* radio programs. For much of the 1980s, he led a trio that featured bassist George Mraz and various drummers. Mraz was replaced by Peter Washington in 1990.

In 1993, Flanagan was awarded the Danish Jazzpar Prize, and in 1996 was selected for a National Endowment for the Arts Jazz Masters Fellowship. In October 2001, Flanagan made his final appearance, in a John Coltrane tribute at the San Francisco Jazz Festival. He died in New York soon after, on November 16, 2001, at the age of 71.

How to Play It

"West Coast Blues" is a Montgomery original that appears on the guitarist's 1960 Riverside album, *The Incredible Jazz Guitar of Wes Montgomery*, which features bassist Percy Heath, drummer Albert Heath, and Flanagan on piano.

Flanagan's solo on "West Coast Blues" reveals the pianist as a master of subtlety. There are subtle rhythmic displacements of phrases from the outset. There are subtle horn-like dynamics within phrases and even subtle horn-like breathing spaces in between phrases. There is the subtle pulling back of certain notes at the end of phrases to sit back on the time.

Flanagan's blues licks and inflections are tasteful and heartfelt, but never gratuitous. His swing feel is snappy yet relaxed. Even his left-hand voicings are subtle in providing long, sustained harmonic beds that color everything; being placed with such precision and delicate touch, they don't steal the limelight.

The phrase "less is more" is a strange paradox. Quantitatively speaking, less is less. But qualitatively speaking, as Flanagan proves, sometimes less is better.

Vital Stats

Pianist: Tommy Flanagan

Song: "West Coast Blues"

Album: *The Incredible Jazz Guitar of Wes Montgomery* (1960)

Age at time of recording: 30

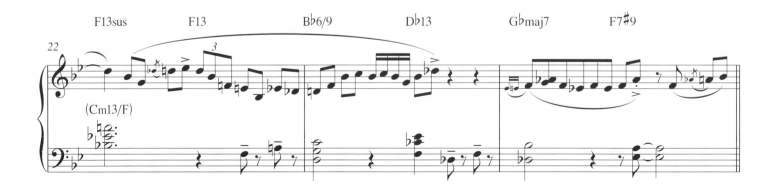

Phineas Newborn Jr.

"In his prime, he was one of the three greatest jazz pianists of all time."

–Leonard Feather

Jazz journalist Leonard Feather once said of Phineas Newborn Jr., "In his prime, he was one of the three greatest jazz pianists of all time." With many now holding Newborn in such high regard, he was surely for many decades one of the most under-recognized musicians in jazz, only in relatively recent years receiving the acknowledgment his playing – and particularly his phenomenal technique – deserved.

Born on December 14, 1931 in Whiteville, Tennessee, Phineas Newborn Jr. came from a musical family. His father, Phineas Newborn Sr., was a blues drummer and his younger brother Calvin a jazz guitarist. Growing up, Newborn learned piano, trumpet, and both tenor and baritone saxophones.

While still in his teens, Newborn played in a successful R&B band with his father and brother, along with bassist Tuff Green, tenor saxophonist Ben Branch, and trumpeter and future boss of Hi Records, Willie Mitchell. From 1947 to 1951, the group was house band at the now famous Plantation Inn Club in West Memphis, Arkansas. The group became B.B. King's band for his first recordings in 1949, when Newborn was just 18 years old, and recorded

© Ted Williams CTSImages

Phineas Newborn Jr.

The Sun Sessions with the legendary blues musician in 1950.

In 1951, the band left West Memphis to tour with Jackie Brenston as the Delta Cats, in support of the R&B singer's record *Rocket 88*, generally considered to be the first-ever rock 'n' roll record. It was the first *Billboard* No. 1 for Chess Records.

From 1956, after serving in the military between 1952 and 1954, Newborn began to perform as a jazz musician in New York City, working with bandleaders Lionel Hampton and Charles Mingus. He also led his own trios and quartets, which contained the likes of Oscar Pettiford, Kenny Clarke, and Philly Joe Jones. In 1956, Newborn recorded his first albums as a leader for RCA Victor, *Here Is Phineas* and *Phineas' Rainbow*. Both were quartet records featuring his brother on guitar. After a third quartet record in 1958, *Fabulous Phineas*, Newborn exclusively released piano trio albums for the rest of his career, starting with *We Three* (1958), which featured drummer Roy Haynes and bassist Paul Chambers. Newborn continued to perform in various other settings, including as a solo pianist in Stockholm in 1958 and Rome in 1959.

After moving to Los Angeles around 1960, Newborn recorded a sequence of six trio albums on the Contemporary label over the 15-year period from 1961 to 1976, the final three with bassist Ray Brown and drummer Elvin Jones. The transcription of "Four" is taken from the second of these six albums, *The Great Jazz Piano of Phineas Newborn* (1963).

During this time, Newborn's career and output were somewhat hampered by ongoing health problems, which perhaps led to his under-appreciation by critics. He made a partial comeback in the late 1970s and early 1980s, but gradually faded from view before his death in 1989. A few years later, The Contemporary Piano Ensemble was formed by pianists Harold Mabern, James Williams, Mulgrew Miller, and Geoff Keezer to pay tribute to a pianist they viewed as one of the all-time greats.

How to Play It

"Four" is a jazz standard composed by saxophonist Eddie "Cleanhead" Vinson in 1954. Authorship is frequently, yet mistakenly, attributed to Miles Davis as he was the first to record the tune, releasing it on his 1956 album *Blue Haze*. Phineas Newborn performed "Four" on his 1963 trio album *The Great Jazz Piano of Phineas Newborn*, released on Contemporary.

Newborn is widely regarded as one of the most technically brilliant pianists in jazz history, and on this recording we hear him performing in his trademark solo style. Newborn delivers an extended solo using immaculate bebop language, executed crisply in double-handed unison two octaves apart, with occasional rhythmic block-chord interjections.

Like Newborn, look to make your left hand as strong and fluid as your right, and listen to and imitate how he uses accents and articulation to propel his phrases forward. His lines are generally legato and quite often end with a pronounced staccato "pop."

Vital Stats

Pianist: Phineas Newborn

Song: "Four"

Album: *The Great Jazz Piano of Phineas Newborn Jr.* (1963)

Age at time of recording: 32

Transcr. Huw White

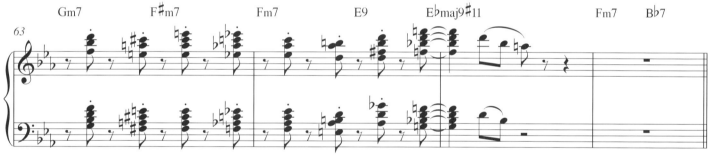

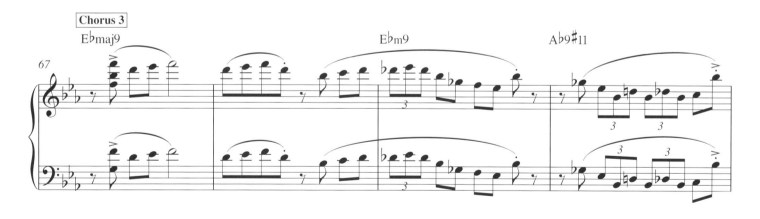

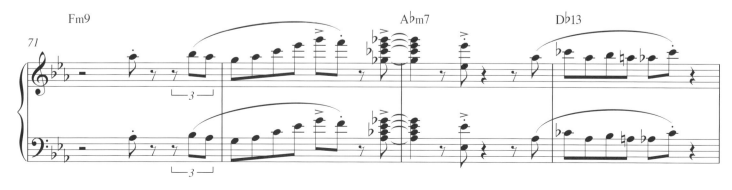

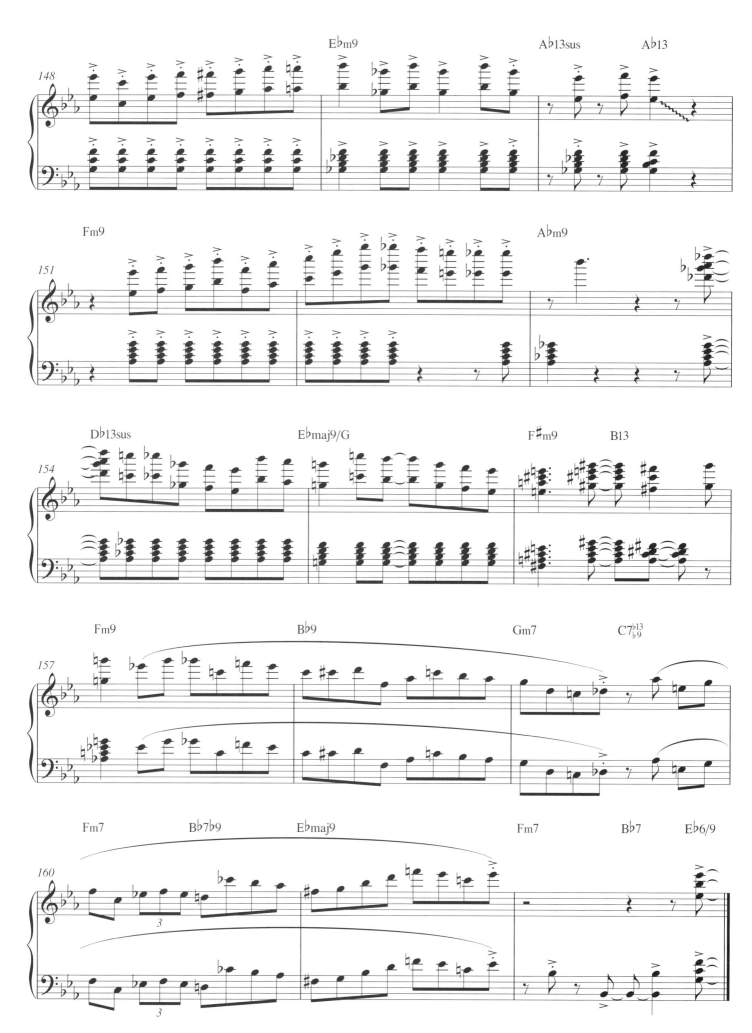

Herbie Hancock

"Music happens to be an art form that transcends language."
–Herbie Hancock

Herbie Hancock has been one of the most significant and progressive jazz musicians in the world for over half a century, with an influence that extends beyond the generic boundaries of jazz. He was a pioneer of post-bop, funk, and electronic music, as well as of the jazz/pop crossover.

© Agencja Fotograficzna Caro / Alamy Stock Photo

Herbie Hancock

Born in Chicago, Illinois on April 12, 1940, Herbert Jeffrey Hancock studied classical piano from the age of seven. Considered a child prodigy, he performed the first movement of Mozart's Piano Concerto No. 26 with the Chicago Symphony Orchestra at the age of 11. Through his teens, Hancock developed his ear and astonishing sense of harmony by assimilating the harmonic concepts of arrangers such as Clare Fischer, composers such as Ravel, and fellow jazz pianists such as Bill Evans and the lesser known Chris Anderson, who took Hancock on as a student.

In 1960, Hancock began working with trumpeter Donald Byrd and tenor saxophonist Coleman Hawkins in Chicago, earning himself a reputation

that led to recording sessions with Oliver Nelson and Phil Woods. In 1962, Hancock's first album for Blue Note, *Takin' Off* (from which the transcription of Hancock's solo on "Driftin'" is derived), caught the attention of Miles Davis, who in May 1963 hired Hancock as pianist for a band that became one of the greatest ensembles in jazz history: Miles Davis's Second Great Quintet.

The band's rhythm section, comprised of bassist Ron Carter, 17-year-old drummer Tony Williams, and pianist Hancock developed a level of innovative interaction that completely transformed the role of the jazz rhythm section. The level of complexity they reached eventually gave birth, in the late 1960s,

to perhaps one of the purest and freest forms of harmonic and rhythmic expression in jazz: "time, no changes."

During a prolific period, Hancock also recorded dozens of sessions for the Blue Note label, under his own name and as a sideman with the likes of Wayne Shorter, Bobby Hutcherson, Sam Rivers, and Freddie Hubbard. His albums *Empyrean Isles* (1964) and *Maiden Voyage* (1965) in particular became key exponents of the post-bop idiom, while albums written for larger ensembles – such as *Speak Like a Child* (1968) – showed off Hancock's compositional skill.

In the 1970s, Hancock ventured into electronic music. Between 1971 and 1973, he released three highly

HERBIE
HANCOCK
TAKIN'
OFF
FREDDIE HUBBARD
DEXTER GORDON
BUTCH WARREN
BILLY HIGGINS
STEREO
84109 BLUE NOTE

experimental records that became known as the "Mwandishi" albums, after Hancock temporarily adopted the Swahili name meaning "writer."

Soon after, influenced by the music of Sly Stone, Hancock formed the jazz-funk fusion band The Headhunters. The band's eponymous debut album, released in 1973, was a major hit with mainstream pop audiences, and was followed by a string of successful releases and further ventures into the pop world by Hancock.

In 1983, Hancock had a popular hit with the Grammy Award-winning single "Rockit." It was the first single to feature scratching, and became a worldwide anthem in 1980s hip-hop culture, reaching No. 8 on the U.K. charts.

Alongside his electronic, funk, and pop explorations, Hancock continued to record and tour more traditional jazz music. During the late 1970s and early 1980s, he toured and recorded with the V.S.O.P. quintet, which featured all the members of the 1960s Davis quintet except the original leader, with Freddie Hubbard on trumpet instead. In 1978,

Hancock recorded a duet with Chick Corea and also released a solo acoustic piano album simply titled *The Piano* (1979).

Through to the present day, Hancock has continued to write, record, and tour in a vast array of settings, even delving into film work. In 1986, he performed and acted in the film *'Round Midnight*. He also wrote the score/soundtrack, for which he won an Academy Award for Original Music Score.

In 1990, Hancock joined with Jack DeJohnette, Dave Holland, and Pat Metheny for the *Parallel Realities* tour. In 1994, together with Carter, Williams, Shorter, and trumpeter Wallace Roney, Hancock recorded *A Tribute to Miles,* winning a Grammy for best group album. *The New Standard* (1995) found Hancock and an all-star band – including John Scofield, DeJohnette, and Michael Brecker – interpreting pop songs from a range of eras and styles. In 2005, Hancock released *Possibilities*, an album of duets with mainstream pop stars such as Paul Simon, Sting, and Christina Aguilera, receiving two Grammy nominations.

In 2007, Hancock released *River: The Joni Letters*, a tribute to the work of his longtime associate Joni Mitchell, with vocals contributed by Norah Jones, Tina Turner, and Corinne Bailey Rae. In the 2008 Grammys, *River* won both Album of the Year and Best Contemporary Jazz Album, perhaps best summing up the achievements of Hancock's extraordinary career – bringing jazz into the mainstream while maintaining personal artistic integrity.

How to Play It

"Driftin'" is a Hancock original written for his 1962 debut album on Blue Note, *Takin' Off*. It finds Hancock in laid-back yet direct form, sitting right back on the beat, particularly during his long, boppy 16th-note runs that frequently outline his superimposed reharmonizations.

The solo is bluesy throughout, with lots of crushed grace notes and idiomatic ornaments. Hancock's technique in the block chord sections is reminiscent of his counterpart in Miles Davis's First Great Quintet, Red Garland, with repeated chords in the left hand and octave melodies in the right, occasionally filled out into chords. Hancock's touch is much weightier than Garland's, though, with plenty of bluesy slides and a signature Hancock tremolo thrown in, and typically full left-hand voicings throughout. Like Hancock, try to sit back, dig in, and swing hard.

Vital Stats

Pianist: Herbie Hancock
Song: "Driftin'"
Album: *Takin' Off* (1962)
Age at time of recording: 22

Transcr. Huw White

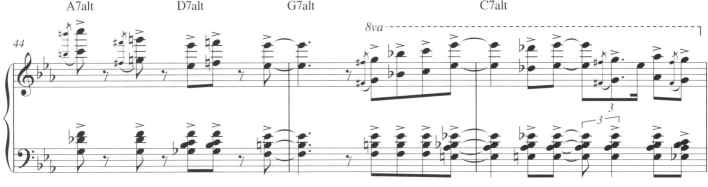

Oscar Peterson

"If you have anything to say of any worth then people will listen to you."

–Oscar Peterson

Courtesy Wikimedia Commons

Oscar Peterson

Oscar Peterson is considered by many to have been one of the greatest, if not the greatest, jazz pianist in history. In a 1976 interview, guitarist Joe Pass claimed: "The only guys I've heard who come close to total mastery of their instruments are Art Tatum and Peterson." In a career lasting more than 60 years, Peterson played thousands of concerts all over the world, released over 200 records, and won countless awards.

Born on August 15, 1925 in Montreal, Canada, Oscar Emmanuel Peterson was raised by West Indian parents in a neighborhood saturated by the flourishing jazz culture of the early 20th century. At the age of five, Peterson began working hard at trumpet and piano. By seven, he directed all his attention to the piano, initially under the tutelage of his father and sister.

Peterson's childhood piano teachers were steeped in a classical pedagogy directly inherited from Franz Liszt, and it was the young student's persistence in practicing scales and classical etudes daily that developed his virtuosity. Glimpses of Peterson's classical heritage, and the influence of composers from Bach to Rachmaninov, would eventually be traceable throughout his recorded career. Alongside his classical studies, Peterson was captivated by jazz and learned to play ragtime and boogie-woogie.

At 14 years of age, after winning a national music competition organized by the Canadian Broadcasting Corporation in 1940, Peterson dropped out of school and became a professional pianist, working for a weekly radio show and playing at hotels and music halls. His early influences were Teddy Wilson, Nat King Cole, James P. Johnson and, most significantly, Art Tatum. Peterson modeled his musicianship on Tatum during the 1940s and 1950s.

In 1949, Peterson's career advanced significantly when jazz impresario Norman Granz introduced him during a Jazz at the Philharmonic show in New York's Carnegie Hall. Through his relationship with Granz, Peterson began playing with major jazz artists, and made numerous duo performances

and recordings with a long list of musicians, most significantly with bassist Ray Brown, with whom he would strike one of the longest known musical partnerships in jazz.

In the early 1950s, Peterson expanded his duo with Brown to a trio. After playing and recording with various third members, including drummer Charlie Smith and guitarists Irving Ashby and Barney Kessel, Peterson eventually settled on guitarist Herb Ellis in 1953. Over the next five years, the trio of Peterson, Brown, and Ellis became one of the most celebrated in jazz, claiming their finest recording to be 1956's *Oscar Peterson at the Stratford Shakespearean Festival*.

When Ellis left the group in 1958, Peterson and Brown believed he was irreplaceable. In 1959, drummer Ed Thigpen was brought in and the new trio lasted until 1965, releasing a number of classic albums on Verve such as *Night Train* (1963). Throughout the 1960s in particular, Peterson often added a star frontline player to his trio, resulting in a number of quartet albums, such as *Oscar Peterson Trio + One* (1964), featuring trumpeter Clark Terry.

From 1965–1970, Peterson performed with a new trio featuring bassist Sam Jones and drummer Louis Hayes, who was later replaced by Bobby Durham. Peterson formed another trio in the 1970s, with guitarist Joe Pass and bassist Niels-Henning Ørsted Pedersen. Cast in the mold of the Peterson/Brown/Ellis trio, the group made a number of festival appearances and recordings and won a 1974 Grammy for Best Jazz Performance by a Group for *The Trio*. In 1974, Peterson added British drummer Martin Drew; this quartet toured and recorded extensively around the world.

In the 1980s, Peterson played in duos with Herbie Hancock and his protégé Benny Green, and in the 1990s and 2000s he recorded several albums, accompanied by a combo, for the Telarc label. Although greatly hindered by ill health, Peterson continued to perform into the early 21st century.

Peterson won countless awards throughout his career, including eight Grammys, most notably the Grammy for Lifetime Achievement in 1997. Oscar Peterson died at his home in Mississauga, Ontario on December 23, 2007 at the age of 82.

How to Play It

"C-Jam Blues" is a jazz standard written by Duke Ellington in 1942. Peterson performed it on his 1963 album *Night Train*, released on Verve.

Peterson's solo is a typical mixture of blues riffs, bebop lines, and block-chord passages, propelled forward by insistent and mostly syncopated left-hand comping with occasional boogie-woogie references. A master of all these techniques, Peterson effortlessly weaves in and out of them, the whole time maintaining a driving, playfully urgent sense of swing.

He frequently uses repeated rhythmic riffs and melodic motifs to build tension before suddenly releasing long, adventurous lines. Try to pick out the subtle accents and articulations within Peterson's lines that help shape and propel them forward.

Vital Stats

Pianist: Oscar Peterson
Song: "C-Jam Blues"
Album: *Night Train* (1963)
Age at time of recording: 37

By Duke Ellington
Copyright © 1942 Sony/ATV Music Publishing LLC in the U.S.A.
Copyright Renewed
This arrangement Copyright © 2016 Sony/ATV Music Publishing LLC in the U.S.A.
All Rights Administered by Sony/ATV Music Publishing LLC, 424 Church Street, Suite 1200, Nashville, TN 37219
Rights for the world outside the U.S.A. Administered by EMI Robbins Catalog Inc. (Publishing) and Alfred Music (Print)
International Copyright Secured   All Rights Reserved

C-Jam Blues

Duke Ellington

"It don't mean a thing if it ain't got that swing."

–Duke Ellington

In a career spanning half a century, in which he led his own orchestra from 1923 to his death in 1974, Duke Ellington is considered to have played a key role in elevating the public perception of jazz to be an art form on par with other traditional musical genres. The most recorded jazz composer of all time, he was eventually awarded a posthumous Pulitzer Prize in 1999 in recognition of his achievements.

Edward Kennedy "Duke" Ellington was born on April 29, 1899 in Washington, D.C. Both his parents were pianists and at the age of seven, Ellington began taking piano lessons, later studying harmony and learning to read sheet music. While in his teens, inspired by local ragtime pianists and an encounter with James P. Johnson, he dropped out of school and began playing gigs around Washington. In late 1917, Ellington's first group, The Duke's Serenaders, began playing private balls and parties around the area.

Before long, Ellington moved to Harlem, but discovered a highly competitive emerging jazz scene that was tough to crack, despite help from stride pianist Willie "The Lion" Smith. Eventually, in September 1923, Ellington gained what would become a four-year engagement at the Hollywood Club on Broadway, with Elmer Snowden and his Black Sox Orchestra. When Snowden left the group

in early 1924, Ellington took over as bandleader, making eight records that year and receiving his first composing credits. Duke Ellington and his renamed Kentucky Club Orchestra grew to ten players, including Sidney Bechet for a while. With the help of Ellington's unconventional arrangements, they began to develop a uniquely distinctive "Harlem" sound.

In October 1926, Ellington made a career-advancing agreement with agent-publisher Irving Mills, allowing him to record prolifically on a host of labels, giving Ellington a great deal of popular recognition. In December 1927, Ellington secured an engagement at Harlem's Cotton Club. Weekly radio broadcasts from the club gave Ellington national exposure. Around the same time, Ellington's recording of "Creole Love Call" with Adelaide Hall became a worldwide sensation, giving Ellington his first hit record. Soon afterward, Ellington's film work began with *Black and Tan* (1929), in which he played the hero "Duke."

During the depression of the early 1930s, which struck the record industry hard, radio exposure helped maintain popularity as Ellington and his orchestra began to tour both domestically and overseas, allowing him to release "Mood Indigo" (1930), "Sophisticated Lady" (1933), "Solitude" (1934), and "In a

Courtesy Wikimedia Commons

Duke Ellington

Sentimental Mood" (1935). *Symphony in Black* (1935), a short film featuring Ellington's "A Rhapsody of Negro Life," introduced Billie Holiday and won an Academy Award. In 1937, Ellington returned to the Cotton Club, releasing "Caravan" that year and "I Let a Song Go Out of My Heart" the next.

In 1939, Ellington began to develop an important musical relationship with Billy Strayhorn, with whom he started to share the orchestra's arranging, conducting, rehearsing, and pianistic duties. Strayhorn's "Take the 'A' Train" was a hit in 1941 and became the band's new theme. Other key figures in the early 1940s were double bassist Jimmy Blanton and saxophonists Ben Webster and Johnny Hodges.

Throughout the 1940s, Ellington wrote longer works. *Black, Brown and Beige* debuted at Carnegie Hall on January 23, 1943, initiating an annual series of concerts there over the next four years. *Jump for Joy*, a full-length musical, debuted on July 10, 1941 at the Mayan Theater in Los Angeles. A Broadway production of Ellington's *Beggar's Holiday*, his sole book musical, premiered on December 23, 1946 under the direction of Nicholas Ray.

Despite the rise in popularity of small-group bebop after the war, Ellington continued touring with his orchestra until 1950. In 1951, Ellington suffered a significant loss of personnel. By 1955, after three years of recording for Capitol, Ellington found himself without a record label. However, his appearance at the Newport Jazz Festival led to one of only five *Time* magazine cover stories ever dedicated to a jazz musician; recordings of the show became Ellington's best-selling album. *Ellington at Newport* (1956) was the first release in a new recording contract with Columbia Records that yielded several records over subsequent years, including *Such Sweet Thunder* (1957), leading to an increase in touring once again.

The late 1950s saw Ella Fitzgerald record her *Duke Ellington Songbook* on Verve with Ellington and his orchestra, an acknowledgment of the significant position Ellington's repertoire had come to occupy within American culture. Around this time, Ellington and Strayhorn began scoring for film soundtracks, such as *Anatomy of a Murder* (1959) and *Paris Blues* (1961), which featured Paul Newman and Sidney Poitier as jazz musicians.

In the early 1960s, Ellington embraced recording with younger musicians such as Coleman Hawkins and John Coltrane (both for Impulse), and participated in a session with Charles Mingus and Max Roach that yielded the album *Money Jungle* (United Artists), from which the transcription of Ellington's solo on "Caravan" is derived.

The first of Ellington's Sacred Concerts was given its premiere at San Francisco's Grace Cathedral in September 1965. Described by Ellington as "the most important thing I have ever done," the Sacred Concerts were an attempt to fuse Christian liturgy with jazz. After multiple performances, the Second and Third Sacred Concerts followed in 1968 and 1973. Other recordings toward the end of Ellington's career include his only album with Frank Sinatra, entitled *Francis A. & Edward K.* (1967).

Ellington won a huge list of awards in his career, including the Grammy Lifetime Achievement Award in 1966 and a posthumous Pulitzer Prize in 1999. Duke Ellington performed his final major concert at Northern Illinois University on March 20, 1974. He died two months later, on May 24, 1974, at the age of 75.

How to Play It

"Caravan" is a jazz standard that was composed by Juan Tizol and first performed by Duke Ellington in 1936. Ellington recorded it again in 1962 with bassist Charles Mingus and drummer Max Roach for the 1963 release *Money Jungle* (United Artists).

"Caravan" finds Ellington in some deliberately dissonant, rhythmically jarring territory. From the first entry he uses spiky, accented interjections to explore diminished harmony using the full range of the piano, with high octaves in the right hand and low rumblings in the left. There are touches of minor blues riffs and boogie-woogie throughout, but primarily this solo is all about the rhythmic interplay between the pianist's two hands.

Ellington juxtaposes passages where both hands are in rhythmic unison, either in melodic riffs or block chords, with sections where spiky chords are bounced back and forth between each hand, creating syncopations and polyrhythms. At the first bridge, Ellington performs brisk augmented arpeggios across the piano by passing groups of notes in between each hand. This solo forms a great exercise in rhythmic coordination and interplay.

Vital Stats

Pianist: Duke Ellington
Song: "Caravan"
Album: *Money Jungle* (1963)
Age at time of recording: 64

Transcr. Huw White

McCoy Tyner

"When I don't have feelings, I don't play."

–McCoy Tyner

McCoy Tyner

McCoy Tyner is considered to be one of the most original and influential jazz pianists of the last 50 years, particularly for his role in John Coltrane's Classic Quartet, and as a pioneer of the quartal harmonic approach and "outside" playing.

Alfred McCoy Tyner was born in Philadelphia on December 11, 1938. Already 13 years old when he began studying piano, within two years music had become the focal point in his life. His early influences included fellow Philadelphian pianist Bud Powell.

Tyner came to public exposure in 1960 when he became the first pianist in Benny Golson and Art Farmer's Jazztet. Shortly afterward, Tyner replaced Steve Kuhn in John Coltrane's group during its extended run at the Jazz Gallery; in 1961, he appeared on the saxophonist's popular recording of "My Favorite Things" for Atlantic Records.

Tyner went on to become a member of what later was known as John Coltrane's Classic Quartet, one of the most important groups in jazz. With a rhythm section completed by Jimmy Garrison on bass and Elvin Jones on drums, Coltrane's Quartet toured almost non-stop between 1961 and 1965 and recorded a number of albums on the Impulse! label, including *Live! at the Village Vanguard* (1962), *Ballads* (1963), *Live at Birdland* (1964), *Crescent* (1964), *The John Coltrane Quartet Plays* (1965), and most significantly, *A Love Supreme* (1965).

While in Coltrane's group, Tyner led a series of recordings for Impulse!, mostly in the trio format. He also appeared as a sideman on many key Blue Note albums during the 1960s. After Tyler's involvement with Coltrane came to an end in 1965, he began rehearsing with a new trio and embarked on a full-time career as a leader. Subsequently, Tyner produced a series of post-bop albums released on Blue Note Records, including *The Real McCoy* (1967) – from which the transcription of his solo on "Passion Dance" is derived – *Tender Moments* (1967), *Time for Tyner* (1968), *Expansions* (1968), and *Extensions* (1970). Soon afterward, he moved to Milestone, continuing his output with *Sahara* (1972), *Enlightenment* (1973), and *Fly with the Wind* (1976), which featured a string orchestra.

Tyner's Blue Note and Milestone recordings built upon the sound world developed in Coltrane's Classic Quartet in a highly original way, sometimes incorporating African and East Asian elements. On *Sahara*, for instance, Tyner performs on koto, a Japanese stringed instrument, as well as piano, flute, and percussion. *Trident* (1975) features Tyner on harpsichord and celeste, in addition to his primary instrument, piano.

Throughout the 1980s and 1990s, Tyner continued to tour and record regularly, often with a trio that included Avery Sharpe on bass and first Louis Hayes, then Aaron Scott, on drums. In this time, he also made two solo records for Blue Note, *Revelations* (1988) and *Soliloquy* (1991). Tyner has continued active through to the present day, recording for the Telarc label and playing with trios that have included musicians such as Charnett Moffett on bass and Al Foster on drums.

How to Play It

"Passion Dance," a Tyner original, was the opening track of the pianist's 1967 Blue Note album *The Real McCoy*, featuring tenor saxophonist Joe Henderson, bassist Ron Carter, and drummer Elvin Jones. It reveals quintessential Tyner, with its modal openness leaving him entirely free to revel in and explore some of his most characteristic devices.

Prominent throughout are plenty of pentatonic phrases that, with the support of his trademark mobile quartal left-hand voicings, are able to shift in and out of the F Mixolydian modal center. This creates dramatic tension and release upon returning home, usually marked by a heavy open fifth in the bass. Countless pianists have since imitated and built upon this style of playing. Occasionally, Tyner deliberately chooses not to follow

his right-hand harmonic excursions with his left, for example in bars 37–40 where he creates even more tension and dissonance by pedaling a harmonically "in" chord in his left hand against a harmonically "out" melodic line.

Tyner executes his eighth notes with a punchy, detached staccato that gives his lines a distinctive driving bounce and joy in amongst the intensity of the fiery, angular runs, harmonic shifts, and superimposed sequences. Also characteristic are Tyner's use of rhythmic ostinati, particularly in instances where he sets up a repeating dotted-quarter rhythm across the beat in his left hand, while continuing to play eighth notes through and against them in his right, or inventing rhythmically grouped motifs to match the cross-rhythm, as in bars 50–54.

The block chords that appear briefly, particularly at the end of the solo, also reveal a trademark rhythmic motif and voicing structure. These two-handed chords are built using a mixture of stacked fourths that move up and down the mode, and "so what" chords, which combine intervals of fourths and thirds.

Vital Stats

Pianist: McCoy Tyner
Song: "Passion Dance"
Album: *The Real McCoy* (1967)
Age at time of recording: 29

1:10

Transcr. Huw White

Fast Swing (♩ = 238)

Cycle 1

"F Mixolydian" modal center throughout

Cycle 2

Passion Dance

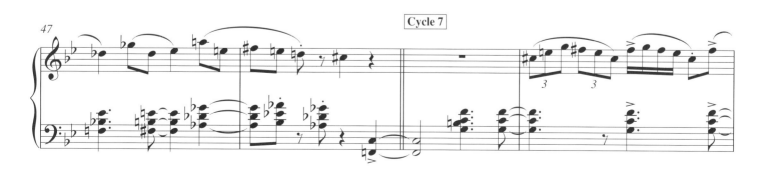

Thelonious Monk

William P. Gottlieb Collection / Library of Congress

Thelonius Monk

"A genius is the one most like himself."
–Thelonious Monk

Thelonious Monk is the second-most recorded jazz composer – after Duke Ellington. Celebrated for his highly individual and unorthodox approach to the piano, Monk was posthumously honored with a Grammy Award for Lifetime Achievement and a Pulitzer Prize in recognition of "a body of distinguished and innovative musical composition that has had a significant and enduring impact on the evolution of jazz."

Born on October 10, 1917 in Rocky Mount, North Carolina, Thelonious Sphere Monk moved to Manhattan, New York City with his family when he was ten years old. Monk started playing the piano at the age of six. Though largely self-taught, he gained musical experience playing organ in church and later studied music theory, harmony, and arranging at the Juilliard School of Music. Monk failed to graduate from high school, and in his late teens began to find work playing jazz.

In the early to mid-1940s, Monk developed his style while house pianist at Minton's Playhouse, participating in after-hours "cutting competitions" with the emerging pioneers of bebop such as Dizzy Gillespie, Charlie Parker, and, later, Miles Davis. Monk's influences included Duke Ellington, James P. Johnson, and other stride pianists.

Monk made his first studio recordings with the Coleman Hawkins Quartet in 1944. His first recordings as leader for Blue Note were made in 1947 (later anthologized on *Genius of Modern Music, Vol. 1*), showcasing his talents as a composer.

In August 1951, New York City police confiscated Monk's cabaret card, without which he was unable to play in any New York venue where liquor was served, severely restricting his ability to perform for a few crucial years. Monk spent those years composing, recording, and performing at theaters and out-of-town gigs.

After recording intermittently for Blue Note from 1947–1952, Monk made several significant albums for Prestige, including collaborations with saxophonist Sonny Rollins and drummers Art Blakey and Max Roach. In 1954, Monk teamed up with Miles Davis to record *Bags' Groove* and *Miles Davis and the Modern Jazz Giants*. That same year, Monk performed and recorded in Paris.

After signing to Riverside, Monk recorded two albums of jazz standards as a means of increasing his profile among a mainstream audience that struggled with his modern compositional and playing style: *Thelonious Monk Plays the Music of Duke Ellington* (1955) and *The Unique Thelonious Monk* (1956). On his following recording in late 1956, *Brilliant Corners*, Monk returned to his own music and this time was well received.

After having his cabaret card restored, Monk relaunched his New York career with a landmark six-month residency

at the Five Spot Cafe beginning in June 1957, leading a quartet with John Coltrane on tenor saxophone. Tunes from a session by the quartet, along with outtakes from a larger group recording featuring saxophonist Coleman Hawkins, were released in 1957 as *Monk's Music*. A 1958 bootleg recording of the quartet live at the Five Spot was issued on Blue Note in 1993, and a recording of the quartet performing at Carnegie Hall that year was released in 2005.

In 1958, Coltrane left Monk to rejoin Miles Davis's group, and the quartet was disbanded. In June 1958, Monk began a second quartet residency at the Five Spot, this time with tenor saxophonist Johnny Griffin (later Charlie Rouse), bassist Ahmed Abdul-Malik, and drummer Roy Haynes.

Two live albums, *Monk in France* and *Monk in Italy*, both recorded in 1961, were the pianist's last Riverside releases. In 1962, Monk signed to Columbia and the following year two new albums were released, *Monk's Dream* and *Criss-Cross*, both featuring his then-regular lineup of tenor saxophonist Charlie Rouse, bassist John Ore, and drummer Frankie Dunlop. Columbia promoted Monk heavily, and *Monk's Dream* became the best-selling record of his lifetime. On February 28, 1964, Monk became one of only five jazz musicians to date to have appeared on the front cover of *Time* magazine.

Monk recorded several more studio albums for Columbia. The transcription of Monk's solo is derived from his solo on "In Walked Bud," a tune written by Monk in 1947 (dedicated to his then-protégé Bud Powell) that appears on the last of these albums, *Underground* (1968).

Monk made several other live albums in the early 1960s, including *Miles and Monk at Newport* (1963) and *Live at the It Club* (1964). By 1964, Ore and Dunlop had been replaced in the quartet by bassist Larry Gales and drummer Ben Riley. Along with Rouse, they remained with Monk for over four years, as his longest-serving band.

Monk made only a small number of appearances during the final decade of his life, and by the mid-1970s had disappeared from the scene. His last studio recordings as a leader were made in November 1971 for the English Black Lion label, near the end of a worldwide tour with the Giants of Jazz, a group that included fellow jazz legends Dizzy Gillespie, Sonny Stitt, and Art Blakey.

Monk died of a stroke on February 17, 1982, in New Jersey, at the age of 64. In 1986, Monk's family co-founded The Thelonious Monk Institute of Jazz in Washington D.C., continuing his legacy.

Vital Stats

Pianist: Thelonius Monk
Song: "In Walked Bud"
Album: *Underground* (1968)
Age at time of recording: 51

How to Play It

Monk wrote "In Walked Bud" in 1947. Based on the chord progression of Irving Berlin's "Blue Skies," it was a tribute to friend and protégé Bud Powell. Monk recorded the tune several times in his career. His final recording of the song was for his 1968 Columbia album *Underground*, featuring tenor saxophonist Charlie Rouse, bassist Larry Gales, drummer Ben Riley, and vocalist Jon Hendricks.

Monk's solo on "In Walked Bud" finds him in familiarly quirky form, in near minimalist territory at times, although as ever playful, surprising, and unpredictable. The first 16 bars are simply four rhythmically displaced and highly percussive variations on a descending, mostly pentatonic motif, with no left-hand work at all. Notice how he leaves space at the end of each phrase for interaction with the snare drum. This is contrasted with a more linear approach to the first "B" section, and a last eight of the first chorus that sees Monk outline the changes more.

The first "A" section of the second chorus sees Monk hammer out a root-note A♭ in the right hand for the whole chorus, with the focus entirely on rhythmic interest, created through the placement of accents that coincide with single-note left-hand bass note interjections – albeit bass notes in an unusually high register. Again, there is space for interaction with the snare, and the following "B" section is linear in contrast before a last eight that sees the changes briefly outlined once more before a bold, punchy blues statement to close.

In Walked Bud

2:10

Medium Up-tempo Swing (♩ = 194)

Chorus 1

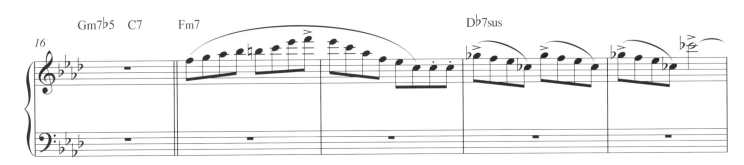

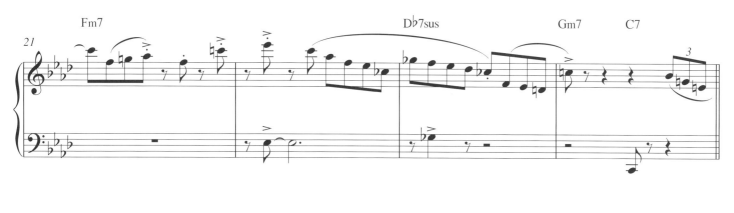

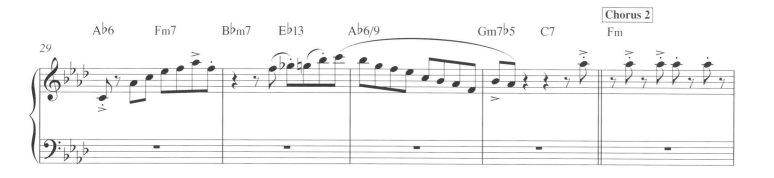

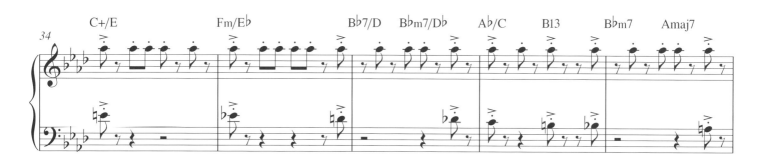

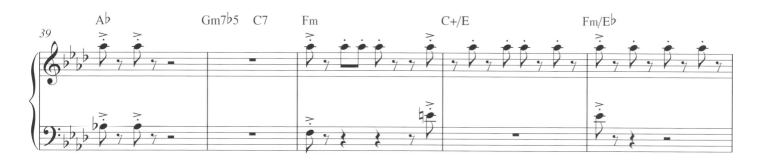

In Walked Bud

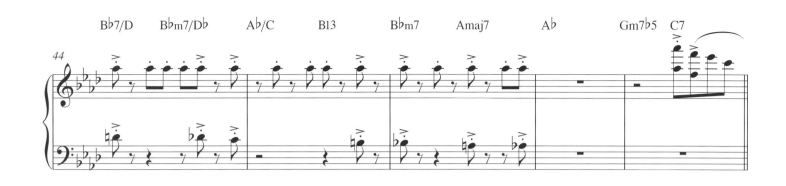

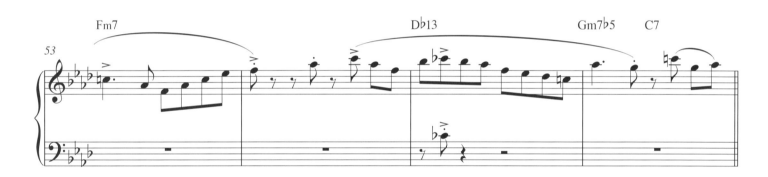

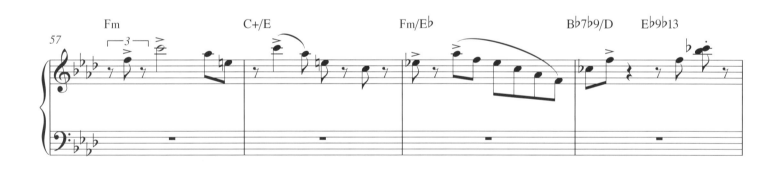

Keith Jarrett

"I am a romantic. I admit it."

–Keith Jarrett

Keith Jarrett is one of the most important pianists in jazz. Renowned for his incredible technique, creativity, and versatility, since the late 1960s he has enjoyed a great deal of success as a group leader and a solo performer in jazz, fusion, and classical music. He is particularly renowned for his completely improvised solo piano concerts. In 2003, Jarrett received the Polar Music Prize, becoming the first winner to this day not to share the prize with a co-recipient. In 2008, Jarrett was inducted into the *Downbeat* Hall of Fame.

Jarrett was born on May 8, 1945, in Allentown, Pennsylvania. After significant early exposure to music, Jarrett developed absolute pitch as a young child and displayed prodigious musical talent. He began piano lessons when he was two years old, and at the age of five he appeared on a TV talent program. Jarrett took intensive classical piano lessons, and gave his first piano recital at the age of seven, playing works by Mozart, Bach, Beethoven, and Saint-Saëns, alongside his own compositions.

In his teens, Jarrett developed a keen interest in the contemporary jazz scene, with Dave Brubeck an early inspiration. He quickly became proficient in playing jazz; fascinated by the music, he turned down an offer to study classical composition in Paris with Nadia Boulanger.

After graduating from high school in 1963, Jarrett moved to Boston to attend the Berklee College of Music, playing cocktail piano in local clubs in his spare time. After a year, he moved to New York City, where he appeared at the Village Vanguard, and was soon hired by Art Blakey to play with the Jazz Messengers.

While playing with the Messengers, Jarrett was spotted by drummer Jack DeJohnette, who recommended him to his own band leader, Charles Lloyd. Jarrett joined the Charles Lloyd Quartet who, with their improvised forms and grooves, were venturing into and expanding upon musical territory being explored by the psychedelic rock bands of the West coast. Their 1966 album *Forest Flower* was one of the most successful jazz recordings of the time. The Quartet's international tours brought Jarrett recognition both in rock and jazz circles, and laid the foundations of a lasting musical bond with drummer DeJohnette. Around the same time, Jarrett began to record as a leader, releasing two trio albums with bassist Charlie Haden and drummer Paul Motian: *Life Between the Exit Signs* (Vortex, 1967) and *Somewhere Before* (Atlantic, 1968).

When the Charles Lloyd Quartet ended in 1968, Jarrett was asked to join the Miles Davis group, where he played Fender Rhodes and organ alongside

Courtesy Photofest

Keith Jarrett

Chick Corea. Jarrett performed on several Davis albums, including *Miles Davis at Fillmore: Live at the Fillmore East* (1970) and *Live-Evil* (1971).

From 1971 to 1976, Jarrett added saxophonist Dewey Redman to the existing trio with Haden and Motian, who had made their final trio album, *The Mourning of a Star*, for Atlantic Records in 1971. The new "American quartet" was often expanded in size and frequently found its members switching to different instruments, with Jarrett heard time and again on soprano saxophone. The group, which explored aspects of free jazz, gospel, and Middle Eastern sounds and heavily featured Jarrett's compositions, recorded two albums for Atlantic Records, one on Columbia, eight on Impulse!, and two on ECM. In the mid- to late-1970s, concurrently with the American Quartet, Jarrett led the "European quartet" with saxophonist Jan Garbarek, bassist Palle Danielsson, and drummer Jon Christensen.

In this period, Jarrett also began to make his first solo recordings on ECM, beginning with *Facing You* (1971). He has continued to record solo piano albums intermittently throughout his career. In 1973, Jarrett began playing totally improvised solo concerts. *Solo Concerts: Bremen/Lausanne* (1973), was awarded Jazz Album of the Year

by *Time* Magazine. *The Köln Concert* (1975) became the best-selling piano recording in history. Others famous solo concert albums include *Paris Concert* (1990), *Vienna Concert* (1991), and *La Scala* (1995), and more recently *Paris/London: Testament* (2008).

In 1983, Jarrett formed a new trio with bassist Gary Peacock and drummer Jack DeJohnette, and released *Standards, Volume 1*. Two more albums, *Standards, Volume 2* and *Changes*, both recorded at the same session, followed soon after. The Standards Trio became one of the most popular and enduring groups in jazz, continuing to record and tour for more than 25 years. While the focus of the Standards Trio was the Great American Songbook, live recordings *Inside Out* and *Always Let Me Go* (both 2001) feature the trio delving back into free jazz.

Since the early 1970s, Jarrett has maintained a parallel career as a classical composer and pianist, recording almost exclusively for ECM Records. In 2004, Jarrett was awarded the Léonie Sonning Music Prize. The award, usually associated with classical musicians and composers, had previously been given to only one other jazz musician – Miles Davis.

How to Play It

"I Fall in Love Too Easily" is a 1944 song by Jule Styne and Sammy Cahn. It was made famous by Frank Sinatra in the 1945 film *Anchors Aweigh* and was nominated for an Academy Award for Best Original Song. Jarrett recorded it with his standards trio, featuring bassist Gary Peacock and drummer Jack DeJohnette, for his 1983 ECM album *Standards, Volume 2*.

Jarrett's solo on "I Fall in Love Too Easily" is a one-chorus masterclass in improvised melody. Note that the transcription intentionally begins in bar 5 of the chorus form, to highlight and draw attention to the ingenious way the trio seems to suspend the mood of the preceding "head" (the song melody chorus) over and into the first four bars of the solo chorus. Listen carefully to the original recording, and you will hear how for a moment time seems to stand still, while in fact the chord changes are still passing underneath, before Jarrett, aided by the perfectly intuitive playing of bassist Peacock, almost tangibly shifts gear into solo mode in bar 5 of the chorus, which is the first bar in the written notation on page 131.

Throughout the solo, there are no pyrotechnics in the right hand, apart from the one impassioned harmonic minor run in bar 20, which is all the more effective due to its isolation. Jarrett simply improvises a highly considered and intentional, sustained and singing melody, with a carefully placed chordal bed in the left hand that provides the simple melodic statements with a harmonic context. It's all about Jarrett's breathtaking poise, touch, and tone, as he effortlessly guides his improvisation back toward the song's original melody.

Keith Jarrett
Standards, Vol. 2
Gary Peacock
Jack DeJohnette

Vital Stats

Pianist: Keith Jarrett
Song: "I Fall in Love Too Easily"
Album: *Standards, Volume 2* (1983)
Age at time of recording: 38

Words by Sammy Cahn
Music by Jule Styne
© 1944 (Renewed) EMI FEIST CATALOG INC. and APPLAUSE AND ENCORE MUSIC
This arrangement © 2016 EMI FEIST CATALOG INC. and APPLAUSE AND ENCORE MUSIC
All Rights for EMI FEIST CATALOG INC. Administered by EMI FEIST CATALOG INC. (Publishing) and ALFRED MUSIC (Print)
All Rights for APPLAUSE AND ENCORE MUSIC Administered by PENNY FARTHING MUSIC (ASCAP) c/o THE BICYCLE MUSIC COMPANY

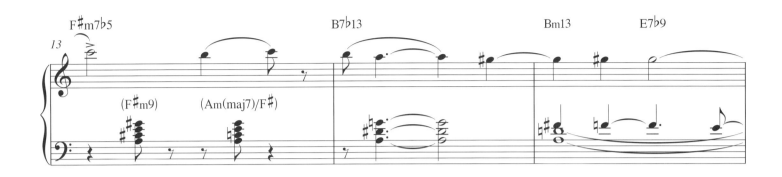

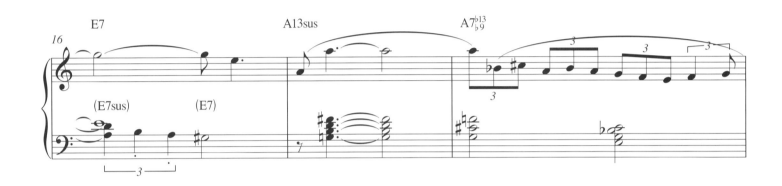

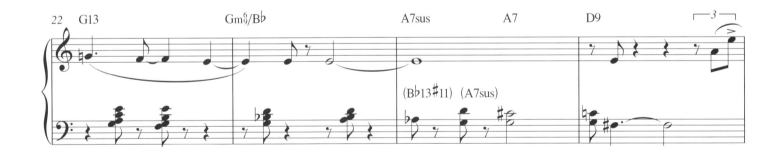

Mulgrew Miller

© Golden Richard / Alamy Stock Photo

Mulgrew Miller

"If you told me when I was in college that I would eventually work with Ron Carter and Tony Williams, I would have thought you were crazy... They were part of what shaped my direction in music."
–Mulgrew Miller

Mulgrew Miller is often described as a key figure in the generation of the "Young Lions" of late-20th century jazz. Growing up into a jazz tradition that included the relatively recent advancements of post-bop, Miller assimilated older influences as well as the style of more current players, particularly McCoy Tyner, creating a style of his own that was incredibly influential among younger players from the late 1980s onward.

Born in Greenwood, Mississippi on August 13, 1955, Mulgrew Miller began learning tunes by ear on the household piano at the age of six. At eight, he started lessons and began playing rhythm and blues at dances, and gospel music at church. Early on, Miller's pianistic influences were Ramsey Lewis, Art Tatum, Erroll Garner, and, most significantly, Oscar Peterson. While in high school, Miller formed his first trio.

After graduating from high school in 1973, Miller gained a band scholarship to Memphis State University, where he was introduced to the music of Wynton Kelly, Bud Powell, and McCoy Tyner. It was there he met his future bandleader, Woody Shaw, at a workshop led by the trumpeter. Miller left college in 1975, taking lessons in Boston with Madame Margaret Chaloff, who had taught many of his favorite pianists. He also spent time playing with saxophonists Ricky Ford and Bill Pierce, before moving to Los Angeles for a year, where he played in clubs and at church.

Toward the end of 1976, Miller was asked to cover for the pianist in the Duke Ellington Orchestra. He ended up touring with the band for three years, until he was recruited by vocalist Betty Carter in January 1980. In 1981, Miller was reunited with Woody Shaw and made his recording debut on the trumpeter's *United*, remaining in Shaw's band for a couple of years. Miller also worked with vocalist Carmen Lundy and saxophonist Johnny Griffin during this time, until he was recruited by Art Blakey's Jazz Messengers in 1983.

Miller made his first recording as a leader with a trio album called *Keys to the City* (1985), the first of several recordings for Landmark Records. After leaving Blakey in 1986, he was a member of Tony Williams's quintet for its entire lifespan until 1993. Simultaneously, Miller began working with his own groups, such as Wingspan and Trio Transition. He was also a sideman with numerous other leaders in the late 1980s, including Steve Nelson, Donald Byrd, Benny Golson, and Wallace Roney. In 1989, he became a founding member of the Contemporary Piano Ensemble. The unusual group, which featured four more piano players, including Geoff Keezer, performed intermittently until 1996.

Miller performed with Golson at the 1990 Moscow International Jazz Festival, and in 1992 toured internationally with the New York Jazz Giants, a septet that featured trumpet player Tom Harrell. In the same year, he released his first album for Novus Records, *Hand in Hand*, and recorded with vocalists Dianne Reeves and Cassandra Wilson. In 1993, Miller began playing and recording with saxophonist Joe Lovano.

From the mid-1990s, Miller began to work less as a sideman and focus more on his own music, although in 1996 he reunited with Williams to appear on the drummer's final recording, *Young at Heart*. Between 1997–1999, he appeared on albums led by Kenny Garrett, Nelson, and a few others.

In 2002, Miller's discography began to grow again, with a series of four concert recordings released over the following years: *Live at The Kennedy Center, Volumes 1 & 2*, with Derrick Hodge (bass) and Rodney Green (drums), and *Live at Yoshi's, Volumes 1 & 2*, with Hodge and Karriem Riggins (drums). Miller also joined bassist Ron Carter's Golden Striker Trio in 2002, and in the mid-2000s joined bassist Dave Holland's band.

From 2005, Miller was the Director of Jazz Studies at the William Paterson University of New Jersey, and in 2008 was Artist in Residence at Pennsylvania's Lafayette College, which had awarded him an honorary doctorate in Performing Arts in 2006.

Miller joined guitarist John Scofield's band in 2010. In the same year, Miller's only solo album, a 2000 concert recording entitled *Solo*, was released. In 2012, selections from a performance in Denmark with the Klüvers Big Band were released under Miller's co-leadership as *Grew's Tune*. In autumn 2012, Miller performed in a piano duo with Kenny Barron, and in the winter of that year he toured Europe with a quintet led by Yusef Lateef and Archie Shepp.

On May 29, 2013, at the age of 57, Miller died after suffering a stroke. He had made more than 15 albums under his own name, and appeared on more than 400 more as a sideman.

How to Play It

"For Openers," by Kenny Garrett, is the first track of the alto saxophonist's 1984 debut album *Introducing Kenny Garrett*, released on Criss Cross. The record features Woody Shaw on trumpet and flugelhorn, Nat Reeves on bass, Tony Reedus on drums, and Miller on piano.

The solo section of Garrett's "For Openers" has similarities to that of McCoy Tyner's "Passion Dance." Like "Passion Dance," it is an up-tempo 4/4 swinger, although a little faster, with 16-bar sections of each chorus effectively "time, no changes" with the F Mixolydian mode as a loose point of return.

This setting helps make the influence of McCoy Tyner on Mulgrew Miller's playing all the more obvious. The left-hand quartal voicings (chords built by stacking intervals of fourths) pioneered by Tyner are prominent, as are plenty of pentatonic lines in the right hand. Miller's highly percussive and bouncy attack in his right-hand lines also recalls Tyner. Miller's occasionally denser left-hand voicings and harmonic side-slips (a tension-and-release device that involves briefly shifting the entire harmonic center by a given interval before returning) are reminiscent of Herbie Hancock's hard-bop approach.

Vital Stats

Pianist: Mulgrew Miller
Song: "For Openers"
Album: *Introducing Kenny Garrett* (1984)
Age at time of recording: 29

1:16

Fast Swing (♩ = 280)

Transcr. Huw White

Chorus 1

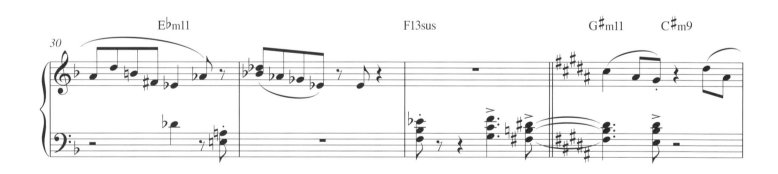

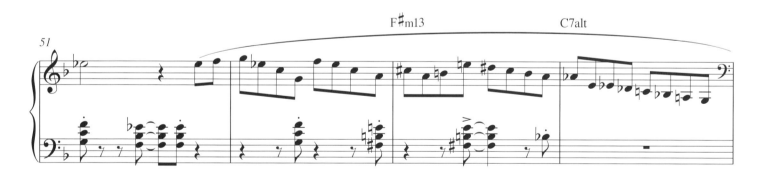

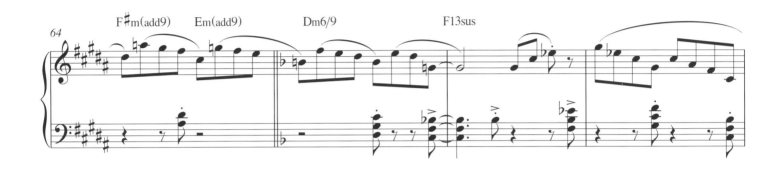

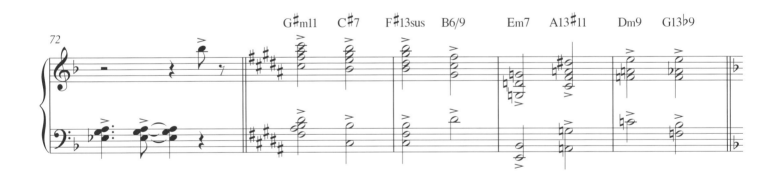

Kenny Kirkland

"It wasn't until I was 13 that it actually caught on for me… I tried to learn something from everyone."

–Kenny Kirkland

Kenny Kirkland's explosive melodies and exciting, distinctive, comping style have been hugely influential on modern pianists over the last 25 years. Equally innovative and skilled in both jazz and pop styles, he played in the most successful groups in both genres, contributing greatly to the development of the early sound of both the Wynton and Branford Marsalis groups, while working with Sting for over ten years.

Born in Brooklyn, New York on September 28, 1955, Kenneth "Kenny" David Kirkland was six years old when he first took to the piano. After receiving a Catholic education, Kirkland enrolled at the Manhattan School of Music, where he studied classical piano performance, classical theory, and composition.

He began playing professionally at the age of 22, when he joined Polish fusion violinist Michal Urbaniak's group for a 1977 European tour. Coincidentally, Kirkland's next major gig was with another Eastern European musician,

© Ray Avery CTSImages

Kenny Kirkland

Czech bassist Miroslav Vitous. Kirkland is featured on Vitous's ECM recordings *First Meeting* (1979) and *Miroslav Vitous Group* (1980). He also appears on Vitous's lesser-known session *Guardian Angels* (1978), which features a 26-year-old John Schofield on guitar.

In 1980, shortly after his stint with Vitous, Kirkland met trumpet player Wynton Marsalis while touring Japan with another trumpeter, Terumasa Hino.

The following year, Kirkland played on Marsalis's eponymous debut album, sharing piano duties with one of his main musical influences, Herbie Hancock. Kirkland was sole occupant of the piano bench in Marsalis's subsequent records *Think of One* (1983), *Hothouse Flowers* (1984), and *Black Codes (From the Underground)* (1985).

After his association with Wynton Marsalis, Kirkland joined the band of the trumpeter's younger brother, saxophonist Branford Marsalis. He went on to record seven albums with Branford's band over a 15-year period, starting with *Scenes in the City* (1983) and ending with *Requiem* (1999), which was dedicated to Kirkland after his tragic passing just months prior to the release. Kirkland also performed on Branford's funk album *Buckshot Lefonque* (1994). In 1992, when Branford Marsalis became bandleader for NBC-TV's The *Tonight Show with Jay Leno*, Kirkland joined him as the band's pianist, showcasing his talents in the mainstream limelight for two years.

Kirkland also ventured into the pop world, most notably with Sting, appearing on six albums with the former star of the Police between 1985 and 1996, including *The Dream of the Blue Turtles* (1985) and *Englishman in New York* (1990).

In 1991, Kirkland released his debut as a leader on GRP Records, *Kenny Kirkland*. The record features various small band combinations of nine musicians, including Branford Marsalis on saxophones, Jeff "Tain" Watts on drums, Don Alias on percussion, and Christian McBride on bass. In the same year, Kirkland recorded the trio album *Thunder and Rainbows* (re-released in 2004 as *Megawatts*) with bassist Charles Fambrough and drummer Watts. In July 1998, Kirkland played on Watts's debut album *Citizen Tain*, in what proved to be one of his final recordings – a few months later, in November 1998, he died of heart failure at the age of just 43.

How to Play It

Kenny Kirkland performed saxophonist Ornate Coleman's "When Will the Blues Leave" on his 1991 album *Kenny Kirkland* (GRP Records). The track features Roderick Ward on alto saxophone, Charnett Moffett on bass, and Jeff "Tain" Watts on drums.

Kenny Kirkland is one of the most popular pianists among today's younger players, celebrated for his vigorous, hard-swinging style. "When Will the Blues Leave" demonstrates how Kirkland's unique improvisational voice is steeped in absorbed tradition, with traits of McCoy Tyner, Herbie Hancock, Thelonius Monk, and Chick Corea coming through.

His driving, weighty eighth-note lines, rich with harmonic content, are reminiscent of Hancock's post-bop work with Miles Davis. His heavier touch, rhythmic playfulness, and angularity occasionally draw Monk to mind – for example, in bars 49–55, where the chordal rhythmic interplay between hands also recalls Duke Ellington.

Kirkland's use of pentatonics, occasional quartal voicings, and harmonic "side-slipping," all demonstrated in bars 33–36, reveal an immersion in the playing style of McCoy Tyner, and similarities to aspects of Chick Corea's approach.

The double-handed open-fourths comping pattern in bars 73–75 is a classic Tyner device. Here Kirkland employs an advanced rhythmic concept with implied underlying groupings of five eighth notes. The dense, weighty voicings that follow in bars 78–83, particularly those with major-triad upper-structure extensions, are very much in the comping style of Hancock.

Kirkland's genius, as with most great players, is in his ability to absorb and assimilate his influences – to speak their language, but to extend it and say something fresh and uniquely his own. In doing so, he himself has become a voice that has impacted a generation of pianists to come.

Vital Stats

Pianist: Kenny Kirkland
Song: "When Will the Blues Leave"
Album: *Kenny Kirkland* (1991)
Age at time of recording: 36

When Will the Blues Leave

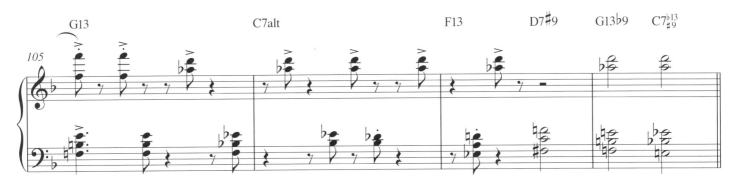

Kenny Barron

Kenny Barron has appeared on hundreds of recordings over the last 50 years, as both a leader and as a sideman, alongside jazz legends such as Ella Fitzgerald, Dizzy Gillespie, and Stan Getz. He continues active in performing, recording, and education today, and is considered one of the most important and influential mainstream jazz pianists and composers since the bebop era.

Born on June 9, 1943 in Philadelphia, the birthplace of many a great jazz musician, Kenny Barron began playing professionally in Mel Melvin's orchestra while still a teenager. In high school, Barron worked with drummer Philly Joe Jones and moved to New York City at age 19. There, he began working with trumpeter Lee Morgan, drummer Roy Haynes, and saxophonist James Moody.

Upon Moody's recommendation in 1962, Barron landed his first major gig as pianist with the Dizzy Gillespie Quartet, where he gained an appreciation for Latin and Caribbean rhythms. After five years with Gillespie, Barron went on to play with Freddie Hubbard, Stanley Turrentine, Milt Jackson, Buddy Rich, and Yusef Lateef.

In the early 1970s, Barron balanced touring with studies to earn a B.A. in Music from Empire State College. By 1973, he had joined the faculty at Rutgers University as professor of music. He remained on faculty until 2000, mentoring many rising star talents, including David Sanchez and Terence Blanchard.

In 1974, Barron recorded *Sunset to Dawn* – his first album as a leader for the Muse label, and the first of over 40 recordings he has made to date. In the late 1970s, Barron formed a trio with Buster Williams and Ben Riley that worked alongside Eddie "Lockjaw" Davis, Eddie Harris, Sonny Stitt, and Harry "Sweets" Edison.

Throughout the 1980s, Barron worked with tenor saxophonist Stan Getz, touring with his quartet and recording several albums, including the Grammy-nominated *People Time*. He also co-founded the quartet Sphere, along with bassist Buster Williams, drummer Ben Riley, and saxophonist Charlie Rouse. Sphere expounded upon music by Thelonious Monk and recorded several albums for Polygram.

Barron's recordings for Verve have earned him nine Grammy nominations, beginning in 1992 for *People Time*, a duet with Getz, and most recently for *Freefall* in 2002. His other Grammy-nominated records include *Night and the*

"You learn, many times, by just observing... You don't have to play everything you know all the time."

–Kenny Barron

City (1998), a duet with bassist Charlie Haden, and *Wanton Spirit* (1994), a trio recording with Roy Haynes and Haden (from which the featured transcription of Barron's solo on "Take the Coltrane" is derived).

Kenny Barron has continued to perform and record through to the present day, most recently collaborating with bassist Dave Holland to create *The Art of Conversation* (2014, Impulse). Barron currently teaches at the Juilliard School of Music, where his latter-day piano students have included young talents such as Earl MacDonald, Harry Pickens, and Aaron Parks.

Barron frequently wins jazz critics' and readers' polls, including in *Downbeat*, *Jazz Times*, and *Jazziz* magazines. He has been named best pianist six times by the Jazz Journalist Association and in 2009 was inducted into the American Jazz Hall of Fame.

How to Play It

Kenny Barron performed Duke Ellington's blues "Take the Coltrane" (written 30 years earlier for the album *Duke Ellington & John Coltrane*) on his 1994 trio album *Wanton Spirit* (Verve), which featured bassist Charlie Haden and drummer Roy Haynes.

"Take the Coltrane" finds Barron in playful form, with rhythmically and harmonically quirky phrases from the start. Barron's articulation is unique, somehow weighty yet delicate and bouncy, with his swung eighth-note lines almost staccato at times.

Barron seems determined to do anything but resolve to a regular F7 chord at the top of the form, maintaining a slight feeling of tension and angularity throughout the solo. In contrast, he is happy to "run the changes" more during the turnaround end of the form, often with traces of classic bebop language, such as in bars 21–22.

In a solo very much led by melodic improvisation, the left-hand voicings are functional yet minimal. Barron's left-hand comping style here is reminiscent of Red Garland or Wynton Kelly, with sparse chords placed largely staccato on the offbeats, particularly on the "and" of beats 2 and 4, oftentimes just outlining the third and the seventh of the harmony. There is the odd McCoy Tyner-style quartal voicing thrown in, particularly to support harmonically "outside" melodic passages, such as in bars 49–52. In this section, Barron uses a descending, harmonically parallel pentatonic sequence in the right hand to add interest over the otherwise static F7 harmony.

Barron superimposes his own improvised harmonic movement over the static F7 harmony in bars 61–63, with his melody simply outlining a chain of dominants, each in a syncopated rhythmic grouping that propels the music forward despite the remoteness from the original harmonic structure. In bars 105–107, Barron creates interest in his melodic line through rhythmic motifs and rhythmic displacement. In this instance, a descending figure of four eighth notes is repeated three times, each starting in a different place in the bar.

See if you can spot the mischievous "hats off" to Coltrane's famous tune "Giant Steps," which explores the relationship between three key centers a major third apart: B major, E♭ major and G major.

Vital Stats

Pianist: Kenny Barron
Song: "Take the Coltrane"
Album: *Wanton Spirit* (1995)
Age at time of recording: 52

Transcr. Huw White

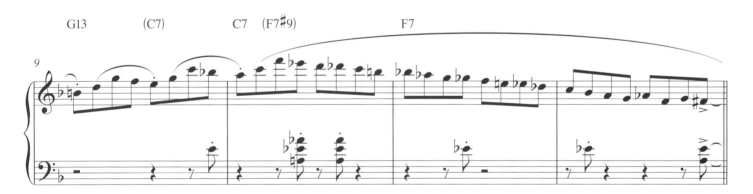

Take the Coltrane

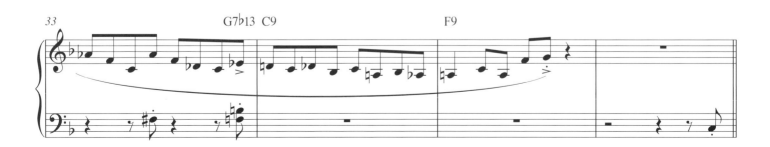

Take the Coltrane

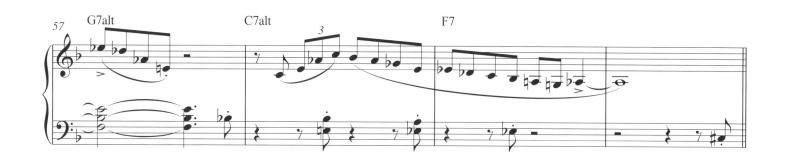

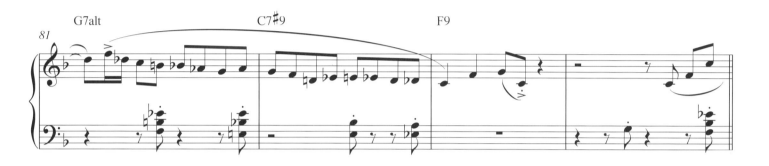

Take the Coltrane

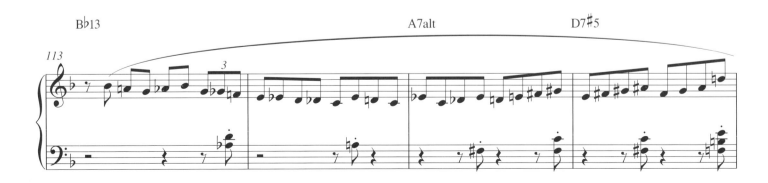

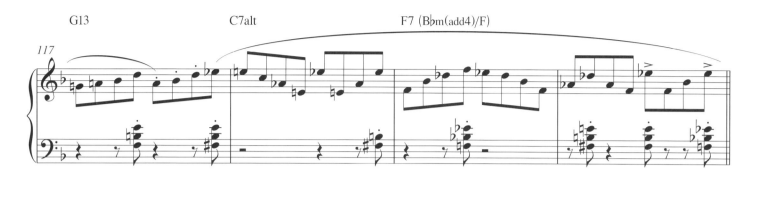

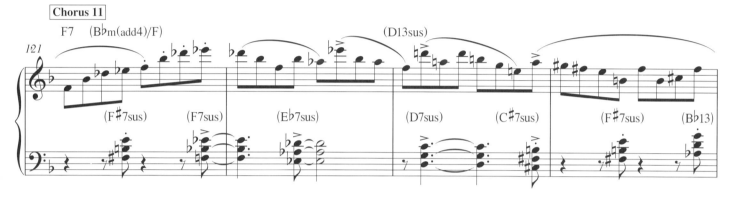

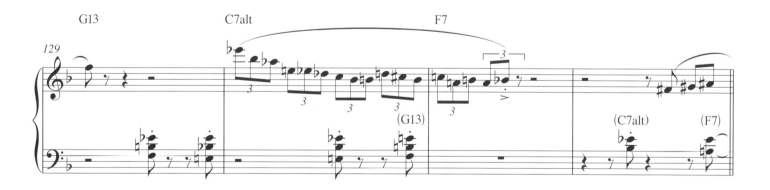

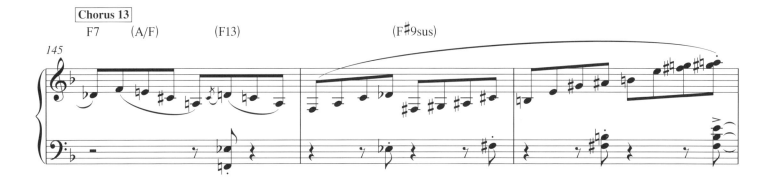

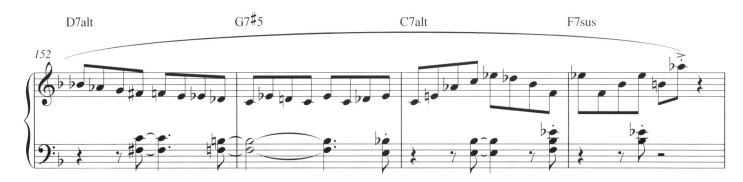

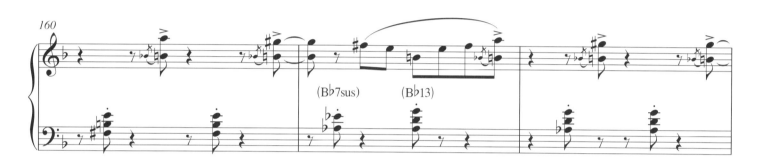

Take the Coltrane

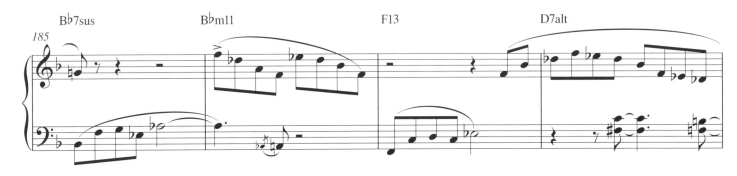

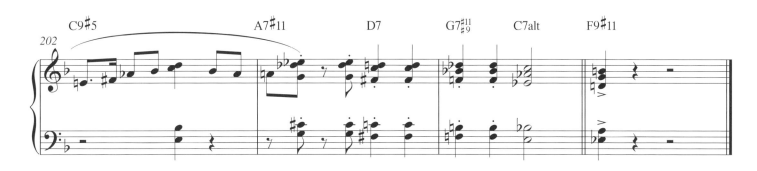

Brad Mehldau

Brad Mehldau is one of the most popular and influential jazz pianists of the present day, winning *Downbeat*'s Readers Poll piano award seven times since 1999. He won the 2006 Miles Davis Prize for "jazz artists who have made significant artistic and innovative contributions to the genre," and has been nominated for five Grammy Awards, including Best Jazz Instrumental Solo on "Blame It on My Youth" from *The Art of the Trio Vol. 1* in 1998. It is this solo that is featured in the transcription here.

Bradford Alexander "Brad" Mehldau was born on August 23, 1970, in Jacksonville, Florida. As a child, he first listened to and imitated pop and rock music on the radio, beginning classical piano lessons at the age of ten. By his teens, Mehldau was listening to jazz artists such as John Coltrane and Oscar Peterson, and he began playing in his high school jazz band. From the age of 15 until he graduated, he had a weekly club gig, and in his junior year at school he won Berklee College's Best All Round Musician Award for school students.

After graduating, Mehldau moved to New York City in 1988 to study jazz and contemporary music at The New School. He studied under pianists Fred Hersch and Kenny Werner and recorded and toured internationally while still a student, assimilating the style of his primary influences Wynton Kelly and McCoy Tyner, while beginning to develop his own sound. In 1993, Mehldau began to attract attention touring with saxophonist Joshua Redman. In the same year, he made his first released recordings

Brad Mehldau

"Any music that is strong will speak to us in different ways at different points in our lives, and will never truly grow irrelevant."
–Brad Mehldau

as a co-leader, *New York-Barcelona Crossing*, comprised of selected takes from a concert in Barcelona with saxophonist Perico Sambeat.

Mehldau graduated from The New School in 1993 and formed his first long-term trio with bassist Larry Grenadier and drummer Jorge Rossy the following year. In 1995, Mehldau recorded his first album as sole leader, *Introducing Brad Mehldau*, receiving critical acclaim. He later recorded *The Art of the Trio Vol. 1*, the first in a series of five groundbreaking albums the trio would record on Warner Bros. over the next five years, documenting the trio's artistic development and helping to establish Mehldau's reputation as a leading figure in jazz. These important records revealed Mehldau to have a formidable technique and a bravely unique artistic voice steeped in jazz tradition but not held captive by it. Mehldau also became known for his unusual choice of material, mixing

standards, originals, and re-workings of popular songs such as Radiohead's "Exit Music (For a Film)" and Nick Drake's "River Man."

Mehldau continued to work as a sideman, in 1996 recording the first of several albums with saxophonist Lee Kontiz and bassist Charlie Haden, and in 1999 recording two albums with Charles Lloyd. During this period Mehldau continued to tour with his trio, and became established on the international festival scene, appearing at the Montreal, Montreux, and North Sea Jazz Festivals.

Mehldau's interest in 19th-century German composers influenced his first solo piano release in 1999, *Elegiac Cycle*. In the following year, *Places* was released, containing solo and trio compositions based on the pianist's experiences of traveling the world.

In 2001, Mehldau scored his first soundtrack, for the French film *Ma femme est une actrice*. In the same year, he began playing with legendary saxophonist Wayne Shorter, recording the Grammy Award-winning *Alegría* with him a couple of years later. In 2002, Mehldau recorded *Largo*, which saw his trio enlarged by instruments more associated with the rock and classical traditions, as well as electronic production. The experimental *Largo* is one of Mehldau's best-selling albums to date.

Another trio session in 2002 resulted in *Anything Goes* (released 2004), and *House on Hill* (released 2006). A solo piano recording from a 2003 concert, *Live in Tokyo*, was released in 2004 as Mehldau's first album for Nonesuch Records.

In the summer of 2004, Mehldau toured Europe in a band that included Joshua Redman and guitarist Kurt Rosenwinkel. That autumn, Mehldau formed a new quartet, with saxophonist Mark Turner, bassist Grenadier, and drummer Jeff Ballard. Ballard replaced Rossy in Mehldau's trio the following year, and the new trio released their first record *Day Is Done* (2005). The same year, Mehldau premiered a song cycle written for classical singer Renée Fleming after a commission from Carnegie Hall, and also began recording and touring with guitarist Pat Metheny.

Another Village Vanguard recording, *Brad Mehldau Trio Live*, was recorded in 2006, notably including 1995 mainstream hit "Wonderwall" by rock band Oasis. That year, Mehldau also played on saxophonist Michael Brecker's final album, *Pilgrimage*, and made another solo recording released as *Live in Marciac* in 2011.

In March 2007, Mehldau premiered his first piano concerto in Paris, and in 2009 began a two-year curatorship of London's Wigmore Hall jazz series. *Highway Rider*, recorded the same year, added a 28-piece orchestra to Mehldau's trio and guest musicians. Two further trio albums were recorded in 2008 and 2011, *Ode* and *Where Do You Start*.

During 2010–11 Mehldau was the first jazz musician to hold Carnegie Hall's Richard and Barbara Debs Composer's Chair. In 2012, Mehldau and the Orpheus Chamber Orchestra performed his *Variations for Piano and Orchestra on a Melancholy Theme* in Europe and the U.S.

In 2013, Mehldau began touring his latest project, "Mehliana," a synth-heavy and largely improvised multi-keyboard and drum duo with Mark Guiliana. *Mehliana: Taming the Dragon*, was released in February 2014, receiving a Grammy nomination the following year.

How to Play It

"Blame It on My Youth" is a jazz standard written by Oscar Levant and Edward Heyman in 1934. Mehldau performed it on his 1997 Warner Bros. release *The Art of the Trio Vol. 1*, featuring bassist Larry Grenadier and drummer Jorge Rossy.

The solo on "Blame It on My Youth" reveals the maturity and intellect behind Mehldau's musicianship, and the wealth of technical and theoretical ability at his disposal. Throughout the solo, we hear how Mehldau is able to juxtapose understated, heartfelt lyricism reminiscent of Bill Evans in one moment, with sudden complex rhythmic and harmonic drama of his own unique conception the next. A typical Medhlau device is to intensify the rhythmic or dynamic mood to emphasise a particularly expressive re-harmonization.

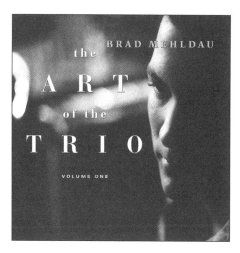

For example, the sudden accented, hard-swinging 16th notes at bar 49 bring out the drama of the tritone substitution into the bridge, starkly contrasting with the tranquility of the resolution of the preceding section.

The solo is largely a right-hand linear exploration set against a rich harmonic bed in the left hand, with both hands always working together harmonically. Mehldau has a unique ability to create rhythmic complexity within his melodies, and stretch the time to the point where the lines between describable theoretical parameters and free rhythmic expression are blurred. Yet his execution and articulation are always so precise and intentional, and there is always such a clear point of resolution, that his playing never sounds fluffy or pretentious. Mehldau's playing remains truly improvisational, exploratory, and sensitive to the moment, while rooted in assimilated tradition and intellectual thought and study.

Vital Stats

Pianist: Brad Mehldau

Song: "Blame It on My Youth"

Album: *The Art of the Trio, Vol. 1* (1997)

Age at time of recording: 26

Transcr. Huw White

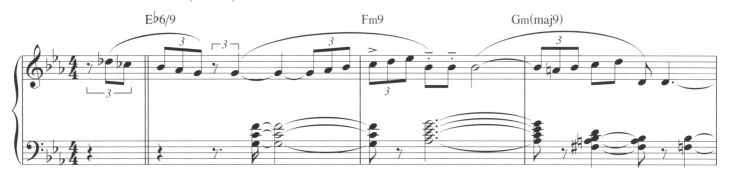

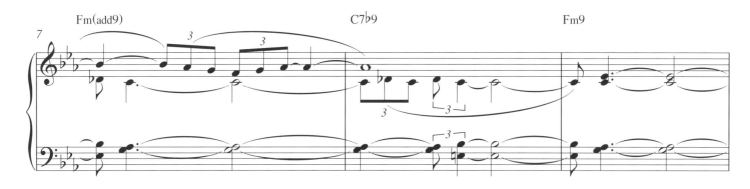

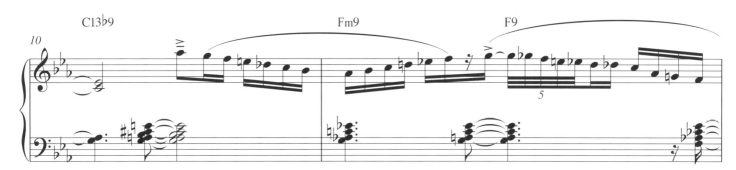

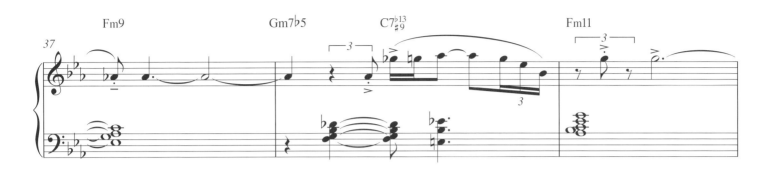

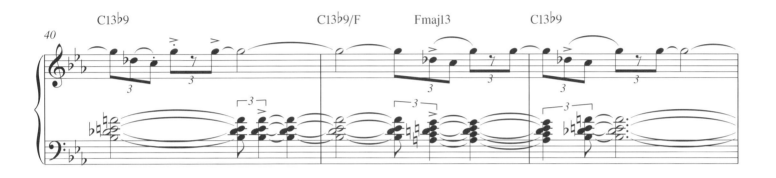

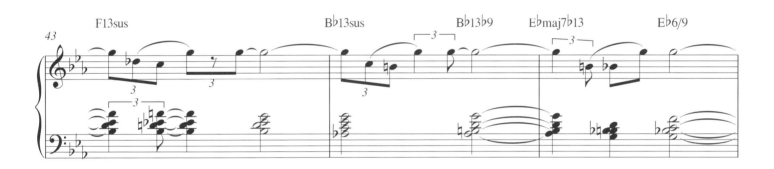

Chick Corea

"You don't have to be Picasso or Rembrandt to create something. The fun of it, the joy of creating, is way high above anything else to do with the art form."
–Chick Corea

Courtesy Photofest

Chick Corea

Chick Corea has been one of the most important voices in jazz piano over the last 50 years. As a member of Miles Davis's band in the 1960s, he played a key role in the birth of the electric jazz fusion movement and has continued to explore a wide range of musical styles through to the present day.

Born in Chelsea, Massachusetts on June 12, 1941, Armando Anthony "Chick" Corea is of Italian and Spanish descent, a heritage that can be traced in his music throughout his career, most notably in his 1976 album *My Spanish Heart* and in his most famous composition, "Spain" (1972).

Corea's father, a jazz trumpeter, introduced him to the piano at the age of four. Surrounded by jazz, Corea was influenced early on by bebop pianists such as Bud Powell and Horace Silver. At the age of eight, Corea took up drums, which undoubtedly influenced his highly percussive approach to piano playing. At the same age, he started taking lessons from concert pianist Salvatore Sullo, and developed a keen interest in classical music and composition.

Corea began playing gigs while still in high school. After graduating, he moved to New York to study music education at Juilliard, but soon quit and began to seek a career on the music scene. He launched his professional career in the 1960s, gigging with the likes of Cab Calloway, trumpeter Blue Mitchell, and Latin musicians such as Herbie Mann, Willie Bobo, and Mongo Santamaría. His first album as a leader was *Tones for Joan's Bones* in 1966, two years before the release of his influential trio album *Now He Sings, Now He Sobs* in 1968, with Roy Haynes on drums and Miroslav Vitouš on bass.

Corea replaced Herbie Hancock in Miles Davis's band in September 1968 and appeared on a string of seminal albums, including *Filles de Kilimanjaro* (1968), *In a Silent Way* (1969), and *Bitches Brew* (1970). Davis's rhythm section of Corea, Dave Holland, and Jack DeJohnette fused elements of free jazz improvisation and rock music, giving Corea the opportunity to experiment with electric instruments, namely the Fender Rhodes electric piano.

In 1970, Corea and Holland left to form their own free jazz group, Circle, which featured multi-reed player Anthony Braxton and drummer Barry Altschul. The group, which explored atonality and

The Chick Corea New Trio

Past, Present & Futures

extended techniques, recorded on both Blue Note and ECM.

In April 1971, Corea recorded solo sessions for ECM released as *Piano Improvisations, Vols. 1 & 2*. Shortly afterward, Corea began to focus on new Latin-jazz fusion group Return to Forever, with the release of an eponymous debut album that featured vocalist Flora Purim, flautist/saxophonist Joe Farrell, bassist Stanley Clarke, drummer/percussionist Airto Moreira, and Corea himself back on Fender Rhodes. It was the group's second album, *Light as a Feather* (1972), that featured Corea's most famous composition, "Spain." The group later included, at various times, drummers Tony Williams and Lenny White and guitarists Bill Connors and Al Di Meola, remaining active in bursts and in various guises through to the present day.

Alongside Return to Forever, Corea also started recording a series of duet albums for ECM with vibraphonist Gary Burton, including *Crystal Silence* (1972). Over 35 years later, the pair's record *The New Crystal Silence* (2008) won a Grammy award. From the late 1970s onward, various other duet projects have been

a feature of Corea's career, most notably a series of concerts and recordings with pianist Herbie Hancock.

In the 1980s and 1990s, along with bassist John Patitucci and drummer Dave Weckl, Corea developed the Elektric Band and the Akoustic Band. The latter marked a shift in Corea's sound back toward traditional acoustic jazz.

The Chick Corea New Trio, which features bassist Avishai Cohen and drummer Jeff Ballard, released the album *Past, Present & Futures* in 2001. The opening track of the album, "Fingerprints," clearly a hats off to Wayne Shorter's famous minor blues composition "Footprints" (1966), is the song from which Corea's solo has been transcribed.

Corea has remained active through to the present day. Since the turn of the century he has won a Grammy for his jazz fusion album *Ultimate Adventure* (2006), become increasingly involved with contemporary classical music, and continued to tour the world with both Return to Forever and the Five Peace Band, which features guitarist John McLaughlin.

How to Play It

"Fingerprints" by Chick Corea is the opening track on his 2001 album *The Chick Corea New Trio: Past, Present & Futures* (Concord), with Avishai Cohen (bass) and Jeff Ballard (drums).

"Fingerprints" is more than a hats off to Wayne Shorter's "Footprints." Although there is no real reference to the melody, it shares a similar harmonic and metric structure. Both are 12-bar C minor blues, with unusual harmonic turnarounds in the last four bars of the form that contrast the otherwise relatively static harmony, creating a point of departure and return, a natural tension and release on every chorus. Both are in a 6/4 meter but explore polyrhythms, meaning the meter can be felt in a number of different ways: for example in 2, with the emphasis on beats 1 and 3; in 3, with the emphasis on beats 1, 3, and 5; or in 4, with the emphasis on each dotted-quarter note.

Corea weaves in and out of these and other various time feels, frequently implying them and creating cross-rhythms through carefully placed accents and rhythmic groupings in his right-hand phrases or through his left-hand chord placement. Corea's rhythmic placement is incredibly precise and detailed, requiring great poise and often giving birth to complex syncopations.

In general, Corea plays right on top of the beat, bringing about a sense of urgency and drama. His articulation is immaculate, juxtaposing long, chromatic legato phrases with staccato interjections and block chords.

Vital Stats

Pianist: Chick Corea

Song: "Fingerprints"

Album: *Past, Present & Futures* (2001)

Age at time of recording: 60

Transcr. Huw White

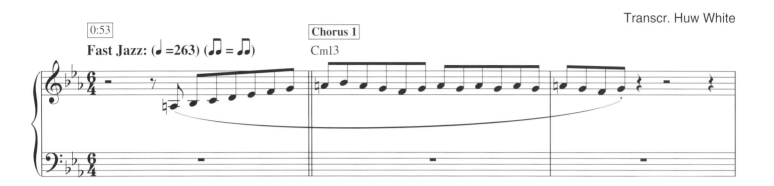

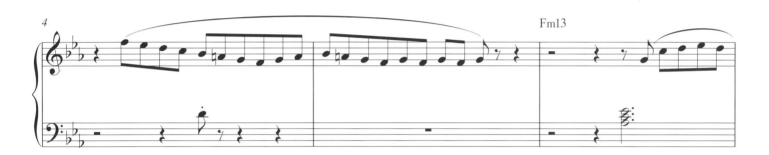

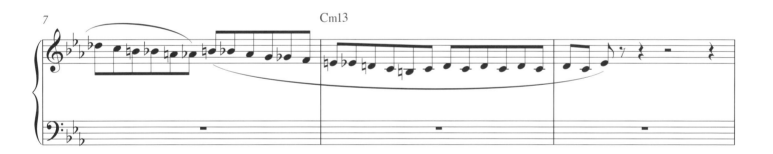

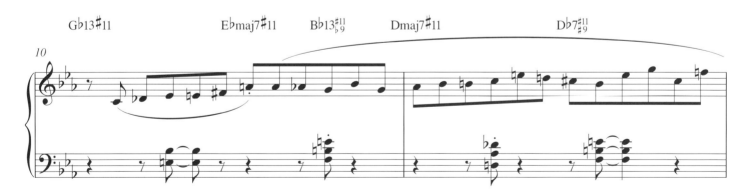

By Chick Corea
Copyright © 2013 Crystal Silence Music
This arrangement Copyright © 2016 Crystal Silence Music
All Rights Administered Worldwide by Songs Of Kobalt Music Publishing
All Rights Reserved   Used by Permission

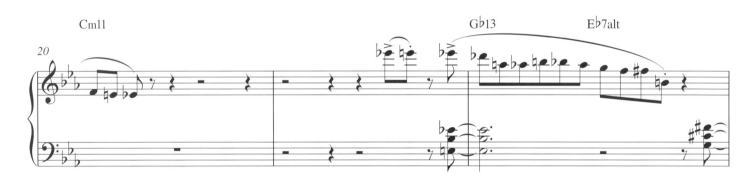

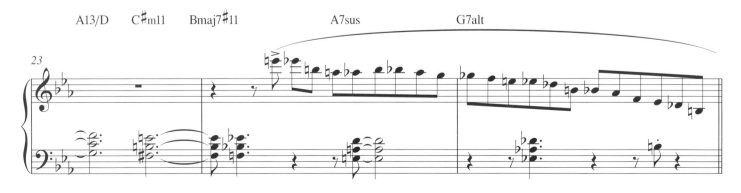

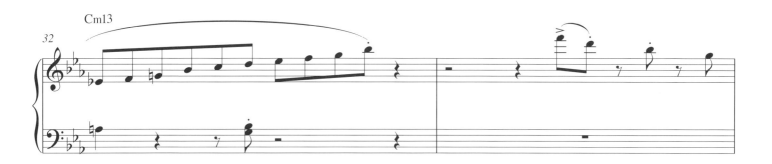

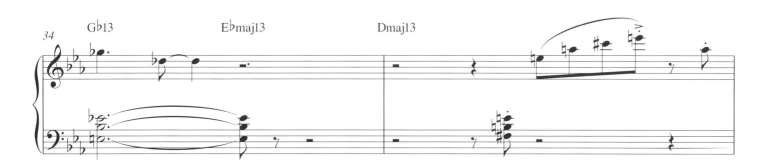

Fingerprints

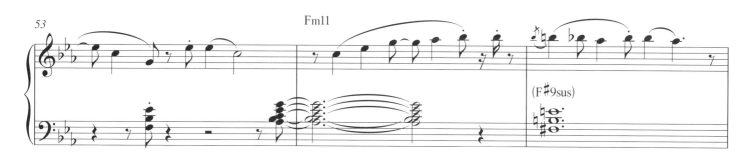

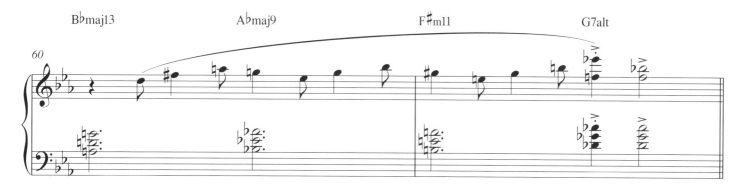

Joey Calderazzo

Joey Calderazzo is one of the most popular and accomplished pianists and jazz composers of the present day. He has had long playing and writing relationships with two of the most important and influential tenor saxophonists of the last 40 years, the late Michael Brecker (1987–2005) and Branford Marsalis (1999–present). Calderazzo has recorded nine of his own solo and trio records to date, picking up various Grammys and other honors along the way.

Born on February 27, 1965 in New Rochelle, New York, Joey Calderazzo began his piano studies at the age of seven, inspired by his next door neighbor. He developed quickly in a very musical household, and at 14 became the youngest member of his brother Gene's rock band. When his older siblings enrolled at Boston's Berklee College of Music and switched their allegiance to jazz, Calderazzo followed suit. He set aside the Beatles and Led Zeppelin for Oscar Peterson, Chick Corea, Herbie Hancock, and McCoy Tyner.

In 1987, Calderazzo met Michael Brecker at a clinic. Soon afterward, he found himself being introduced to the jazz world as part of the Michael Brecker Quintet, appearing on two tracks of the the saxophonist's 1988 album *Don't Try This at Home*. Brecker produced and played on Calderazzo's first disc released on Blue Note records, *In the Door* (1990), along with two other tenor saxophonists whom Calderazzo had met in Boston, Jerry Bergonzi and Branford Marsalis.

Joey Calderazzo

"Musically, I like cornering yourself and trying to get out of it."
–Joey Calderazzo

Two more Blue Note albums followed: *To Know One* (1991) with Bergonzi, Marsalis and a rhythm section completed by bassist Dave Holland and drummer Jack DeJohnette; *The Traveler* (1992), which featured two different trios made up of bassists John Patitucci and Jay Anderson, and drummers Peter Erskine and Jeff Hirshfield. *Secrets* (1995) featured Bob Belden's arrangements, which surrounded the trio of Calderazzo, drummer James Genus, and bassist Clarence Penn with a seven-piece ensemble.

Calderazzo's ongoing relationship with Brecker led to him contributing as composer as well as pianist on the saxophonist's *Tales from the Hudson* (1996), and as pianist, composer, and co-producer on *Two Blocks from the Edge* (1998). In the late 1990s, Calderazzo began to work more regularly with Branford Marsalis, touring with the saxophonist's jazz/hip-hop/R&B crossover group Buckshot LeFonque and contributing to its second album, *Music Evolution* (1997).

When pianist Kenny Kirkland died in 1998, Calderazzo was tasked with the tall order of replacing him in the Branford Marsalis Quartet. This led to an intense period of growth for Calderazzo, and the following year the pianist recorded his definitive trio album to date, *Joey Calderazzo* (1999, Columbia), with John Patitucci on bass and Jeff "Tain" Watts on drums.

Since then, he has contributed to a number of Marsalis's albums, including *Contemporary Jazz* (2000) – which won a Grammy for Best Jazz Instrumental Album – *Footsteps of Our Fathers* (2002), *Romare Bearden Revealed* (2003), *Eternal* (2004), *A Love Supreme:*

Live in Amsterdam (DVD, 2004), and *Braggtown* (2006). It's Calderazzo's solo on John Coltrane's "Pursuance," from the Amsterdam DVD, that is featured in the transcription here.

In 2002, Calderazzo released his first solo album, *Haiku*, on Branford Marsalis's label, Marsalis Music, followed by *Amanecer* in 2007. In recent years, Calderazzo has continued to be active as a soloist, trio leader, and member of the Branford Marsalis Quartet. In June 2011, Marsalis and Calderazzo released their first duo album, *Songs of Mirth and Melancholy*, on Marsalis Music, with a world premiere performance on June 29, 2011 in Koerner Hall at the 2011 Toronto Jazz Festival. Calderazzo's latest release, *Joey Calderazzo Trio Live* (May 2013), features the pianist's current trio with bassist Orlando le Fleming and drummer Donald Edwards.

How to Play It

"Pursuance" is the third movement of legendary tenor saxophonist John Coltrane's masterpiece *A Love Supreme*. Originally recorded in 1964 by his celebrated Classic Quartet – consisting of pianist McCoy Tyner, drummer Elvin Jones, and bassist Jimmy Garrison – *A Love Supreme* is considered by many to be Coltrane's greatest achievement, particularly in its successful melding of hard bop with modal and free jazz sensibilities.

This 2003 recording of the suite by the Branford Marsalis Quartet, featuring Eric Revis on bass and Jeff "Tain"

Watts on drums, was captured during a live performance in Amsterdam. It finds pianist Joey Calderazzo in burning form.

Like Tyner, one of his more obvious influences, Calderazzo clearly enjoys the improvisational freedom of forms, with relatively static underlying harmony, which allow the soloist to spontaneously invent harmonic movement rather than be restricted by it. "Pursuance" is a fast minor blues without any complex, prescribed re-harmonizations, allowing the improviser the freedom to embellish, depart from, and return to the original harmony at will and – in this case – at lightning speed.

Tyner's influence is clear across the board, evident in many of Calderazzo's harmonic, rhythmic, and melodic devices. He employs mobile quartal left-hand voicings throughout, creating a strong yet harmonically open underpinning to his right-hand lines. These voicings hint at particular modes or scales, while rarely confining Calderazzo's right hand to a single harmonic option. Quartal voicings can describe a mode more fully by being moved conjunctly up and down the scale. For example, see how the E♭ Dorian mode is described by the left-hand voicings in bars 17–18.

Also similar to Tyner, Calderazzo frequently uses pentatonics as a staple of his melodic line. For example, the opening three phrases of the solo are simply constructed of the first, third, fourth, and fifth of the F minor pentatonic scale.

The frequent harmonic "side-slipping," or shifting of the entire harmonic structure temporarily by a specific tonal distance (most frequently a half step), is another Tynerism. This device

Parallelism is a similar device, and another found frequently in Tyner's playing. In bars 129–133, Calderazzo ends a chorus with a chain of parallel minor 11th chords rising in whole steps (with a couple of half steps thrown in). This creates a great deal of rising tension (literally) and the release is emphatic, with the stark contrast of an explosive high register line launched out of the insistent, mid-register, rhythmic homophony of the previous passage. Incidentally, much of the rhythmic content of that passage is also reminiscent of Tyner – weighty block chords with shifting rhythmic accents, aided by the interplay between sustain and staccato.

While the Tyner influence is undeniable, and made all the more obvious by the repertoire in question, Calderazzo has clearly assimilated traits of other great pianists spanning the 40 years between the two "Pursuance" recordings, resulting in the development his own unique sound. The shape and harmonic content of his lines show glimpses of post-bop Hancock as well as Calderazzo's own predecessor in Branford Marsalis's band, Kenny Kirkland – particularly in the way he interweaves intensely chromatic runs with more open pentatonic and arpeggiated figures. The percussive execution and cleanliness of his melodic attack recalls that of Chick Corea on "Steps" from *Now He Sings, Now He Sobs* (1968), although – like Hancock and Kirkland – Calderazzo digs more heavily in to the piano, using a weighty, accented attack to launch and shape his lines, creating an impressive blend of power, agility, and accuracy.

provides a powerful sense of tension and release when the harmony returns back "home" (or "in") after a passage "outside" the harmony. Bars 94–97 provide a good example of this, with Calderazzo approaching the B♭ minor "home" harmony by hinting at B minor, a half step above, then A minor, a half step below, before resolving back into the tonic B♭ minor key center. He strengthens these statements by frequently using bold pentatonic melodic language belonging to each modal center, thus drawing the ear along with him on his harmonic adventures.

Vital Stats

Pianist: Joey Calderazzo

Song: "Pursuance"

Album: *A Love Supreme: Live in Amsterdam* (2004)

Age at time of recording: 38

Pursuance

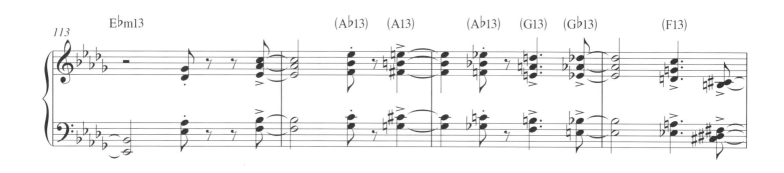

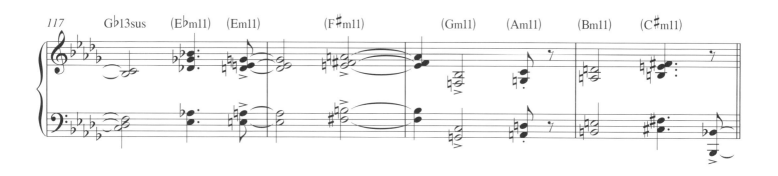

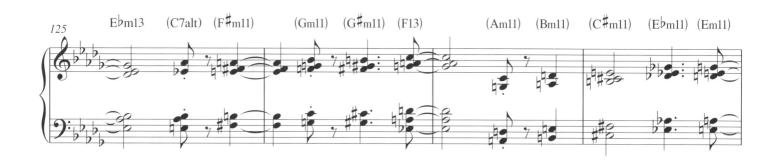

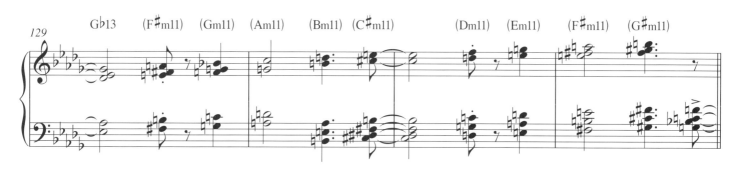

Pursuance

Pursuance

About the Author

Huw White is a jazz pianist, composer, arranger, and orchestrator based in London, UK. Huw graduated from the Royal Academy of Music with a first class degree in jazz piano performance in 2007, after also studying composition, arranging, and classical violin. In his time at the Academy, Huw had the opportunity to play in workshops and masterclasses alongside visiting jazz masters such as Dave Holland, Lee Konitz, and Chris Potter, to name a few. Shortly after graduating, Huw was invited onto the Academy's teaching faculty as a professor of jazz piano. Throughout his 20s, Huw worked primarily as a jazz pianist and composer in and around London, also touring throughout the UK, Europe, and North America, and was described as a "Rising Star" by the BBC during the 2009 London Jazz Festival.

In recent years, Huw has begun to develop a reputation in the UK as a talented and sought-after arranger and composer, fluent in a wide breadth of genres. In 2011, Huw performed one of his original jazz compositions as part of the BBC Proms Series at London's Royal Albert Hall, which was later selected for broadcast on BBC Radio. Huw returned to the Albert Hall in 2013 after he was commissioned to arrange, produce, and direct a new version of the hymn "Amazing Grace" for the opening of the annual Leadership Conference, a major international event run by the largest Anglican Church in Europe, Holy Trinity Brompton. The piece combined complex electronic production with a live rock band, orchestra, marching drummers, pipe organ, and choir, and was transmitted live across multiple venues and online.

Major artists Huw has arranged for in recent years include BBC Sound of 2012 and Mercury Prize Nominee Michael Kiwanuka, and the world's best-selling string quartet Bond. In 2015, Huw worked as an arranger with guitarist and producer Mick Jones (The Clash) on the album *The Third*, by London-based band Kitty Daisy & Lewis, subsequently working as a Musical Director on the group's World Tour. One of the songs Huw arranged for the record, "Baby Bye Bye," received BBC Radio 1's prestigious Single of the Week status upon its release. Also in 2015, Huw scored and directed a number of string arrangements for a live album by the double Grammy Award-winning songwriter Matt Redman, recorded and filmed at the legendary Abbey Road Studios. Later that year, Huw returned to the Royal Albert Hall once more after extending the arrangements to a 300-voice choir and symphony orchestra to accompany Redman live in concert. Most recently, Huw worked alongside multi award-winning pop producer Brian "Danger Mouse" Burton in arranging Michael Kiwanuka's title track for his 2016 album *Love and Hate*.

ARTIST TRANSCRIPTIONS

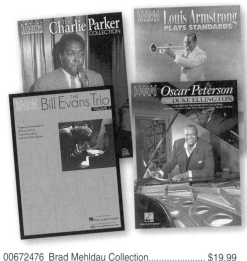

Artist Transcriptions are authentic, note-for-note transcriptions of today's hottest artists in jazz, pop and rock. These outstanding, accurate arrangements are in an easy-to-read format which includes all essential lines. Artist Transcriptions can be used to perform, sequence or for reference.

CLARINET

00672423	Buddy De Franco Collection	$19.95

FLUTE

00672379	Eric Dolphy Collection	$19.95
00672582	The Very Best of James Galway	$16.99
00672372	James Moody Collection – Sax and Flute	$19.95

GUITAR & BASS

00660113	The Guitar Style of George Benson	$14.95
00699072	Guitar Book of Pierre Bensusan	$29.95
00672331	Ron Carter – Acoustic Bass	$16.95
00672573	Ray Brown	$19.99
00672307	Stanley Clarke Collection	$19.95
00660115	Al Di Meola – Friday Night in San Francisco	$14.95
00604043	Al Di Meola – Music, Words, Pictures	$14.95
00672574	Al Di Meola – Pursuit of Radical Rhapsody	$22.99
00125617	Best of Herb Ellis	$19.99
00673245	Jazz Style of Tal Farlow	$19.95
00699306	Jim Hall – Exploring Jazz Guitar	$19.95
00604049	Allan Holdsworth – Reaching for the Uncommon Chord	$14.95
00699215	Leo Kottke – Eight Songs	$14.95
00675536	Wes Montgomery – Guitar Transcriptions	$17.95
00672353	Joe Pass Collection	$18.95
00673216	John Patitucci	$16.95
00027083	Django Reinhardt Antholog	$14.95
00672374	Johnny Smith Guitar Solos	$19.99

PIANO & KEYBOARD

00672338	Monty Alexander Collection	$19.95
00672487	Monty Alexander Plays Standards	$19.95
00672520	Count Basie Collection	$19.95
00113680	Blues Piano Legends	$19.99
00672439	Cyrus Chestnut Collection	$19.95
00672300	Chick Corea – Paint the World	$12.95
14037739	Storyville Presents Duke Ellington	$19.99
00146105	Bill Evans – Alone	$16.99
00672537	Bill Evans at Town Hall	$16.95
00672548	The Mastery of Bill Evans	$12.95
00672425	Bill Evans – Piano Interpretations	$19.95
00672365	Bill Evans – Piano Standards	$19.95
00121885	Bill Evans – Time Remembered	$19.99
00672510	Bill Evans Trio – Vol. 1: 1959-1961	$24.95
00672511	Bill Evans Trio – Vol. 2: 1962-1965	$24.99
00672512	Bill Evans Trio – Vol. 3: 1968-1974	$24.95
00672513	Bill Evans Trio – Vol. 4: 1979-1980	$24.95
00672381	Tommy Flanagan Collection	$24.99
00672492	Benny Goodman Collection	$16.95
00672486	Vince Guaraldi Collection	$19.95
00672419	Herbie Hancock Collection	$19.95
00672438	Hampton Hawes	$19.95
14037738	Storyville Presents Earl Hines	$19.99
00672322	Ahmad Jamal Collection	$22.95
00672564	Best of Jeff Lorber	$17.99

00672476	Brad Mehldau Collection	$19.99
00672388	Best of Thelonious Monk	$19.95
00672389	Thelonious Monk Collection	$19.95
00672390	Thelonious Monk Plays Jazz Standards – Volume 1	$19.95
00672391	Thelonious Monk Plays Jazz Standards – Volume 2	$19.95
00672433	Jelly Roll Morton – The Piano Rolls	$12.95
00672553	Charlie Parker for Piano	$19.95
00672542	Oscar Peterson – Jazz Piano Solos	$16.95
00672562	Oscar Peterson – A Jazz Portrait of Frank Sinatra	$19.95
00672544	Oscar Peterson – Originals	$9.95
00672532	Oscar Peterson – Plays Broadway	$19.95
00672531	Oscar Peterson – Plays Duke Ellington	$19.95
00672563	Oscar Peterson – A Royal Wedding Suite	$19.99
00672569	Oscar Peterson – Tracks	$19.99
00672533	Oscar Peterson – Trios	$24.95
00672543	Oscar Peterson Trio – Canadiana Suite	$10.99
00672534	Very Best of Oscar Peterson	$22.95
00672371	Bud Powell Classics	$19.95
00672376	Bud Powell Collection	$19.95
00672507	Gonzalo Rubalcaba Collection	$19.95
00672303	Horace Silver Collection	$19.95
00672316	Art Tatum Collection	$22.95
00672355	Art Tatum Solo Book	$19.95
00673215	McCoy Tyner	$16.95
00672321	Cedar Walton Collection	$19.95
00672519	Kenny Werner Collection	$19.95
00672434	Teddy Wilson Collection	$19.95

SAXOPHONE

00672566	The Mindi Abair Collection	$14.99
00673244	Julian "Cannonball" Adderley Collection	$19.95
00673237	Michael Brecker	$19.95
00672429	Michael Brecker Collection	$19.95
00672315	Benny Carter Plays Standards	$22.95
00672394	James Carter Collection	$19.95
00672349	John Coltrane Plays Giant Steps	$19.95
00672529	John Coltrane – Giant Steps	$14.99
00672494	John Coltrane – A Love Supreme	$14.95
00307393	John Coltrane – Omnibook: C Instruments	$24.99
00307391	John Coltrane – Omnibook: B-flat Instruments	$24.99
00307392	John Coltrane – Omnibook: E-flat Instruments	$24.99
00307394	John Coltrane – Omnibook: Bass Clef Instruments	$24.99
00672493	John Coltrane Plays "Coltrane Changes"	$19.95
00672453	John Coltrane Plays Standards	$19.95
00673233	John Coltrane Solos	$22.95
00672328	Paul Desmond Collection	$19.95
00672379	Eric Dolphy Collection	$19.95

00672530	Kenny Garrett Collection	$19.95
00699375	Stan Getz	$19.95
00672377	Stan Getz – Bossa Novas	$19.95
00672375	Stan Getz – Standards	$18.95
00673254	Great Tenor Sax Solos	$18.99
00672523	Coleman Hawkins Collection	$19.95
00673252	Joe Henderson – Selections from "Lush Life" & "So Near So Far"	$19.95
00672330	Best of Joe Henderson	$22.95
00672350	Tenor Saxophone Standards	$18.95
00673239	Best of Kenny G	$19.95
00673229	Kenny G – Breathless	$19.95
00672462	Kenny G – Classics in the Key of G	$19.95
00672485	Kenny G – Faith: A Holiday Album	$14.95
00672373	Kenny G – The Moment	$19.95
00672498	Jackie McLean Collection	$19.95
00672372	James Moody Collection – Sax and Flute	$19.95
00672416	Frank Morgan Collection	$19.95
00672539	Gerry Mulligan Collection	$19.95
00672352	Charlie Parker Collection	$19.95
00672561	Best of Sonny Rollins	$19.95
00102751	Sonny Rollins with the Modern Jazz Quartet	$17.99
00675000	David Sanborn Collection	$17.95
00672491	New Best of Wayne Shorter	$19.95
00672550	The Sonny Stitt Collection	$19.95
00672350	Tenor Saxophone Standards	$18.95
00672567	The Best of Kim Waters	$17.99
00672524	Lester Young Collection	$19.95

TROMBONE

00672332	J.J. Johnson Collection	$19.95
00672489	Steve Turré Collection	$19.99

TRUMPET

00672557	Herb Alpert Collection	$14.99
00672480	Louis Armstrong Collection	$17.95
00672481	Louis Armstrong Plays Standards	$17.95
00672435	Chet Baker Collection	$19.95
00672556	Best of Chris Botti	$19.95
00672448	Miles Davis – Originals, Vol. 1	$19.95
00672451	Miles Davis – Originals, Vol. 2	$19.95
00672450	Miles Davis – Standards, Vol. 1	$19.95
00672449	Miles Davis – Standards, Vol. 2	$19.95
00672479	Dizzy Gillespie Collection	$19.95
00673214	Freddie Hubbard	$14.95
00672382	Tom Harrell – Jazz Trumpet	$19.95
00672363	Jazz Trumpet Solos	$9.95
00672506	Chuck Mangione Collection	$19.95
00672525	Arturo Sandoval – Trumpet Evolution	$19.95

HAL•LEONARD CORPORATION

7777 W. BLUEMOUND RD. P.O. BOX 13819 MILWAUKEE, WI 53213

Visit our web site for a complete listing of our titles with songlists at

www.halleonard.com

0216

Prices and availability subject to change without notice.

PLAY PIANO LIKE A PRO!

AMAZING PHRASING – KEYBOARD
50 Ways to Improve Your Improvisational Skills
by Debbie Denke
Amazing Phrasing is for any keyboard player interested in learning how to improvise and how to improve their creative phrasing. This method is divided into three parts: melody, harmony, and rhythm & style. The companion CD contains 44 full-band demos for listening, as well as many play-along examples so you can practice improvising over various musical styles and progressions.
00842030 Book/CD Pack $16.95

BEBOP LICKS FOR PIANO
A Dictionary of Melodic Ideas for Improvisation
by Les Wise
Written for the musician who is interested in acquiring a firm foundation for playing jazz, this unique book/CD pack presents over 800 licks. By building up a vocabulary of these licks, players can connect them together in endless possibilities to form larger phrases and complete solos. The book includes piano notation, and the CD contains helpful note-for-note demos of every lick.
00311854 Book/CD Pack $16.99

BOOGIE WOOGIE FOR BEGINNERS
by Frank Paparelli
A short easy method for learning to play boogie woogie, designed for the beginner and average pianist. Includes: exercises for developing left-hand bass • 25 popular boogie woogie bass patterns • arrangements of "Down the Road a Piece" and "Answer to the Prayer" by well-known pianists • a glossary of musical terms for dynamics, tempo and style.
00120517 .... $9.99

INTROS, ENDINGS & TURNAROUNDS FOR KEYBOARD
Essential Phrases for Swing, Latin, Jazz Waltz, and Blues Styles
by John Valerio
Learn the intros, endings and turnarounds that all of the pros know and use! This new keyboard instruction book by John Valerio covers swing styles, ballads, Latin tunes, jazz waltzes, blues, major and minor keys, vamps and pedal tones, and more.
00290525 .... $12.99

JAZZ PIANO TECHNIQUE
Exercises, Etudes & Ideas for Building Chops
by John Valerio

This one-of-a-kind book applies traditional technique exercises to specific jazz piano needs. Topics include: scales (major, minor, chromatic, pentatonic, etc.), arpeggios (triads, seventh chords, upper structures), finger independence exercises (static position, held notes, Hanon exercises), parallel interval scales and exercises (thirds, fourths, tritones, fifths, sixths, octaves), and more! The CD includes 45 recorded examples.
00312059 Book/CD Pack $19.99

JAZZ PIANO VOICINGS
An Essential Resource for Aspiring Jazz Musicians
by Rob Mullins
The jazz idiom can often appear mysterious and difficult for musicians who were trained to play other types of music. Long-time performer and educator Rob Mullins helps players enter the jazz world by providing voicings that will help the player develop skills in the jazz genre and start sounding professional right away – without years of study! Includes a "Numeric Voicing Chart," chord indexes in all 12 keys, info about what range of the instrument you can play chords in, and a beginning approach to bass lines.
00310914 .... $19.95

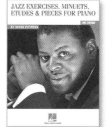

OSCAR PETERSON – JAZZ EXERCISES, MINUETS, ETUDES & PIECES FOR PIANO
Legendary jazz pianist Oscar Peterson has long been devoted to the education of piano students. In this book he offers dozens of pieces designed to empower the student, whether novice or classically trained, with the technique needed to become an accomplished jazz pianist.
00311225 .... $12.99

PIANO AEROBICS
by Wayne Hawkins
Piano Aerobics is a set of exercises that introduces students to many popular styles of music, including jazz, salsa, swing, rock, blues, new age, gospel, stride, and bossa nova. In addition, there is a CD with accompaniment tracks featuring professional musicians playing in those styles.
00311863 Book/CD Pack $19.99

PIANO FITNESS
A Complete Workout
by Mark Harrison
This book will give you a thorough technical workout, while having fun at the same time! The accompanying CD allows you to play along with a rhythm section as you practice your scales, arpeggios, and chords in all keys. Instead of avoiding technique exercises because they seem too tedious or difficult, you'll look forward to playing them. Various voicings and rhythmic settings, which are extremely useful in a variety of pop and jazz styles, are also introduced.
00311995 Book/CD Pack $19.99

THE TOTAL KEYBOARD PLAYER
A Complete Guide to the Sounds, Styles & Sonic Spectrum
by Dave Adler
Do you play the keyboards in your sleep? Do you live for the feel of the keys beneath your fingers? If you answered in the affirmative, then read on, brave musical warrior! All you seek is here: the history, the tricks, the stops, the patches, the plays, the holds, the fingering, the dynamics, the exercises, the magic. Everything you always wanted to know about keyboards, all in one amazing key-centric compendium.
00311977 Book/CD Pack $19.99

HAL•LEONARD®
7777 W. BLUEMOUND RD. P.O. BOX 13819
MILWAUKEE, WISCONSIN 53213
www.halleonard.com

Prices, contents, and availability subject to change without notice.

1115

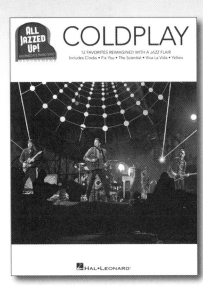

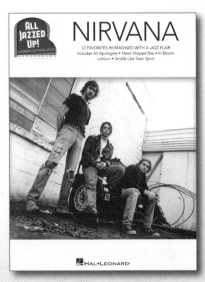
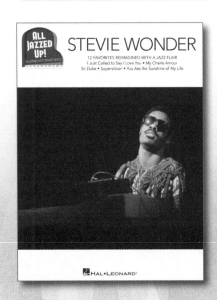